A Life in the Law

A LIFE IN THE LAW

A Woman Lawyer's Life
in Post-World War II Albuquerque, New Mexico

Mary M. Dunlap
with
Mary Kay Stein

SUNSTONE
PRESS

SANTA FE

Sunstone books may be purchased for educational, business, or sales promotional use.
For information please write: Special Markets Department, Sunstone Press,
P.O. Box 2321, Santa Fe, New Mexico 87504-2321.

Book and Cover design › Vicki Ahl
Body typeface › Minion Pro
Printed on acid-free paper
∞
eBook 978-1-61139-306-4

Library of Congress Cataloging-in-Publication Data

Dunlap, Mary M., 1916- author.
  A life in the law : a woman lawyer's life in post-World War II Albuquerque, New Mexico
/ by Mary M. Dunlap, with Mary Kay Stein.
    pages cm
  Includes bibliographical references and index.
  ISBN 978-1-63293-009-5
  1. Women lawyers--New Mexico--Albuquerque--Biography. 2. Women lawyers--New
Mexico--Albuquerque--History. 3. Practice of law--New Mexico--Albuquerque--History.
I. Stein, Mary Kay, 1944- author. II. Title.
  KF373.D86A3 2014
  340.092--dc23
  [B]
                                        2014021964

WWW.SUNSTONEPRESS.COM
SUNSTONE PRESS / POST OFFICE BOX 2321 / SANTA FE, NM 87504-2321 /USA
(505) 988-4418 / ORDERS ONLY (800) 243-5644 / FAX (505) 988-1025

Dedication

With thanks to my brothers
Bob Dunlap and Sheldon Gardner,
Sister Betty Verplank, and all
those who remember our Mother.

Contents

FOREWORD

In 1947, our mother, Minta Mary McDonald Dunlap, left her promising law practice in metropolitan Denver to move to Albuquerque with her husband and growing family. Once in Albuquerque, she became one of only three practicing women lawyers, and was soon in a completely different environment and culture. Instead of the professionally friendly and urban culture of Denver, she encountered a decidedly male-oriented and dominated culture, where women were mostly homemakers.

She recalled that Albuquerque in the late 1940s represented a remarkable mix of cultures, ideas, beliefs, and prejudices. Albuquerque was changing drastically: almost overnight, the once-quiet town had a huge influx of new postwar residents. As was the case throughout the U.S. after World War II, families all over America were on the move, looking for new opportunities, especially in the West and Southwest. Just like in the Depression, when the Dustbowl drove families from the Midwest, postwar Americans were looking for a better life. Many who ended up in Albuquerque had really been heading for a better life on the West coast. Too often they made it only partway, and Albuquerque was the stopping-off place.

The newcomers soon blended in with people whose families had lived in New Mexico since the time of the earliest tribes and the Spanish Conquest and Albuquerque's official founding in 1706—Native Americans, Mexicans, Spaniards, and Anglos. You might even think of this as the formation of one more large tribe along the Rio Grande—more than one civilization arose and fell along the river's banks. New Mexico had seen many peoples and pueblos long before this. One Native American metaphor described this rise and fall as a natural cycle: just as the clouds slowly form, build to a crescendo, then slowly dissipate back to an empty sky, all pueblos or towns rise and then fall, but more would come.

At the end of the 1940s and early 1950s the mesas to the west and the east of Albuquerque were still largely empty, except for a flying service owned by the Black family. This would soon change.

Despite a legal and business culture that was decidedly male and Hispanic, and not generally welcoming to professional women, somehow Mary M. made her way, helped along by a hearty sense of humor and lots of hard work. She needed a great sense of humor because sometimes business as usual in New Mexico could be like living on the dark side of the moon. Cultures and prejudices about gender did clash. She loved to tell the story about a fellow lawyer who drew her aside after a particularly tough session in court to complain, "I can't understand it—outside the courtroom you are so sweet and polite, but when we get to court you cut our *cajones* [translation: balls] off!"

When she first arrived in New Mexico, she couldn't have known that the state would become her permanent home or even imagined she'd be balancing a tricky triangle: a hectic life as a mother of four children, hard work on the family's farm in Corrales, and a challenging law practice. Later came the mental and physical demands of working with Federal Judge Carl A. Hatch. In her 40-plus years in New Mexico, she saw every side of the legal world and some that other attorneys couldn't even imagine, including witchcraft practiced by *curanderas*, tangles with justices of the peace and crooked cops, and even a pair of cases of slavery in the mid-1960s.

In so many ways Minta Mary McDonald Dunlap lived the American Dream. Imagine, for example, a child literally born on a kitchen table in 1916 in Abilene, Kansas, who later learned to read by scanning the newspapers her family used for tablecloths. This same young girl was the first in her family to go to college, and on to law school, making her way with scholarships and many part-time jobs, including waitress, cleaning lady, and courier. Her little town of Eureka, Kansas, helped her as it could. The town was proud of her, and members of several wealthy families gathered clothing so she would have something to wear when she started school at the University of Kansas. She always excelled in school, setting scholastic records that still stand today in her hometown high school, and earned a Phi

Beta Kappa key at the University of Kansas, even while working part-time at all possible jobs, whenever and wherever she could.

Why did she decide to be a lawyer? It could have begun with her grandfather, John James Leonal Kramm. The tall, quiet man took a special liking to Minta Mary, who was a curious and active child. From the beginning, the slight dark-haired girl was different, smart and self-possessed compared to other children around her. Grandpa Kramm liked to take her out under the Kansas night skies to find the Milky Way and to point out the major constellations. He had big plans for her: He wanted her to be a lawyer, but a very particular type, she recalled—a corporate lawyer for the Santa Fe Railway.

After all, it was the railway that made the Manchester Hotel possible, and provided successful careers for her two uncles with the Santa Fe Railroad. Instead, she followed the advice of an early mentor, an old judge in Eureka. The judge told her to remember that the true purpose of and reason for the law was to use it to help everyone, without reservation. She took it to heart and instead of aiming for a partnership in a law firm, established a practice in general law, with an emphasis on poverty law later in her career. She was instrumental in writing the original *New Mexico Children's Code,* served as a Small Claims Court judge, and organized an Equal Employment Opportunity Commission (EEOC) legal team in Dallas that successfully prosecuted one of the largest lawsuits in the federal agency's history, a discrimination case against General Dynamics. Another of her dreams came true when she was admitted to practice before the U.S. Supreme Court.

This book is the result of a small treasure trove of audiotapes Mary M. made while she was recovering after a near-fatal bout with cancer. While she recovered, she lived in Placitas, in the mountains northeast of Albuquerque. For months she stayed in a little rented house that had once been a stagecoach stop.

The crumbling adobe building was down a long and deeply rutted dirt road, nearly impassable in good times and impassable when it rained or snowed. She loved the solitude but also soon became bored, an unusual state for her. Her close friends couldn't understand why she was in the mountains and not in Albuquerque, closer to friends and services. More than one close friend, such as University of New Mexico Professor Dorothy Cline, chided her about "hiding out in the mountains." Professor Cline tried to entice Mary M. back to Albuquerque through letters filled with news of the latest political scandals and intriguing cases, but as she was recovering from a tough bout with gastric cancer, our mother was just not in the mood to jump right back into practice or to see anyone other than close family members. She also said that she needed to have privacy when she was down, and said she "never wanted to go anywhere with my hat in my hand."

The stagecoach stop in Placitas.

As a way to help her pass the time in Placitas, I sent her a tape recorder and a set of blank tapes, and asked her to tell us about her career and clients and Albuquerque in the 1940s, 1950s, and early 1960s. She had so much more to tell, including her work in the later 1960s, 1970s, and 1980s, when she became the lead lawyer with the Equal Employment Opportunity Commission (EEOC) in Dallas and later returned to New Mexico. There was so much territory she never got to and many questions unanswered about those later years. Fate stepped in to stop the story in 1984.

This book is a result of the tape recordings she made while living in Placitas, and we hope readers enjoy it. Perhaps some other young girl or boy facing real challenges and seemingly impossible hurdles will be inspired by her story.

—Mary Kay Stein

1

1947: Welcome to Albuquerque

As our car pulled up to the first stoplight in town on Rio Grande Boulevard, then a one-way street that had yet to get a sewer line, a woman stepped out of a café into the street in front of us. A gunshot blast shook the air, and she fell screaming to the ground. A man shot her again and again, saving one bullet for himself. Then he stuck the gun in his mouth and flew backward like someone had tossed a rag doll.

I pushed my son Sheldon down into the seat, and ducked down under the dash. When we finally looked up, I realized I had witnessed my first murder and suicide. In fact, it was the first real violence I'd ever seen. Meanwhile my son Robert, five, and daughter Mary Kay, three, had calmly slept through it all in the back seat.

Later I learned that this was a husband who had been vainly trying to get back with his estranged wife. He had searched for her all over Albuquerque, with no luck. None of her friends and especially no family members claimed to know where she was. The word was that her husband found her after his minister advised him that she was working as a waitress in a cafe right off Rio Grande Boulevard. The husband waited until his ex-wife got off work and shot her as she walked out the front door.

We read all about the terrible case in the daily paper.

The June 4, *Albuquerque Journal* told the story of the tragedy under the headline:

Parents of Five Children Die in Double Shooting

In a spectacular street shooting, a newcomer to Albuquerque killed his wife and himself at 7:30 am Thursday, on Rio Grande Blvd., a short distance off West Central.

The woman was the mother of five children.

An inquest determined that Ossie Clem Reames, 39, of Jones, Okla., shot his wife to death and then turned the .38 caliber revolver on himself.

The shooting occurred while the wife was enroute to her job as waitress at a West Central café.

The two bodies were found lying on the ground about four feet south of 112 North Rio Grande Blvd., Sheriff's Deputy Ted Kemmer reported.

Bereaved relatives of Mrs. Reames denied a report that a minister's opposition to divorce for the couple led to the tragedy. This eyewitness account of the tragedy was given by Tony Garcia, Rt. 5, who was en route to work at 7:30 am.

"I was sitting on the steps of Old Town Society Hall waiting for a bus when I saw this man (Reames) walking to and fro from the hall to the Old Town School, back and forth.

"I then saw her (Mrs. Reames) come out and they began to argue. He hit her with the butt of a gun and she fell to the ground. She then got up and started running and yelling. He overtook her and shot her once, but she did not fall.

"He then hit her again with the gun butt and she fell. Then he put the gun up to his mouth, but seeing her move he withdrew the gun and shot her again through the head. He then opened his mouth and shot himself.

The *Journal* follow-up story on June 5 had this headline:

Woman Warned Before Slaying

Mrs. Ruth Irene Reames, killed Thursday by her husband who then killed himself, had been advised by officers to remain at home that day until her husband could be found and arrested, it developed Friday. Sheriff Harold Hubbell said his deputies had unsuccessfully searched for Reames all Wednesday night because his wife expected him to arrive in the City and feared for her life.

This was our welcome to Albuquerque, which would be our home for the next 40 years. My three children and I had driven down from Denver to find a home, following my husband Robert, who was a bacteriologist who had been transferred from Wadsworth Veterans Hospital in Denver to the Veterans Administration Hospital Lab in Albuquerque. I was very reluctantly leaving behind lots of friends, a new home in Lakewood, and my new law practice.

It was a long trip from Denver, and we had driven straight through, down old Highway 85, through Taos, then Santa Fe, down La Bajada Hill, past Algodones and Bernalillo, and finally to Albuquerque. The country was beautiful, with a huge blue sky, and mostly empty mesas and fields. In those days there were few places to stop along the highway for more than gas, so we brought our own picnic lunch, or that is, what was left of it. Somewhere in northern New Mexico, in the rear view mirror I noticed white shapes sailing out behind our car. These were the slices of bread from our picnic sandwiches—my little son and daughter in the back seat had devised a way to amuse themselves by opening up the sandwiches, eating the insides and sailing the bread out the back windows.

Not long before we drove into the middle of the shooting at the stoplight on Rio Grande Boulevard, I had stopped in Bernalillo to telephone my husband to let him know we were nearly there. The closest phone I could find was in Rosie's Bar in Bernalillo, which was then a tiny town just north of Albuquerque. It was early morning and Rosie's was the only place open. I went inside the bar while my three children waited in the car. Several shaggy old fellows sitting around over their beers heard me talking on the telephone to my husband at the VA Hospital. As I was leaving, they called out, "Lady, we're sure sorry about your husband being in the hospital—and you with that carload of kids to raise by yourself!" This gave me a good feeling about New Mexico, and, as the next hours showed, there would be few dull days ahead.

After this unlikely beginning, I grew to love New Mexico, with its startling natural beauty, skies like no other place on earth, along with its varied cultures and rich history. I came to respect the integrity of its customs and beliefs. I have long had a love affair with New Mexico, not always requited. As with all such great affairs, it has had mighty peaks and valleys, and it certainly didn't begin with love at first sight.

Before I came to New Mexico, my idea of the state fit neatly with Agnes Morley Cleaveland's statement that New Mexico was 'great for men and mules, but hell on women and horses.' Agnes was the author of a memoir, *No Life for a Lady*, set on a ranch in the Datil Mountains in western New Mexico. After nearly 40 years in New Mexico, I haven't entirely retreated from that position.

I want to relate with love and affection some of the adventures I have had as an early-day woman lawyer in our state. I wouldn't have missed a minute of it.

2

My First Trip to New Mexico

Our shocking episode on Rio Grande Boulevard actually happened during my *second* visit to New Mexico. I first traveled to the state the year before, in 1946, driving down by myself from Denver in our little Pontiac coupe. An elderly client in Denver had asked me to investigate the mysterious death of her son in an auto crash on old, narrow two-lane Highway 66, close to Grants, New Mexico.

The problem, my client explained, was that the state policeman who had investigated the accident had filed two conflicting reports. The first report said that the young man had been driving west, with his arm outside the car window, when a lumber truck traveling east in the other lane veered across the highway, crashed into the young man's car, severing his arm and throwing the car into the ditch. The young man bled to death before help could arrive—although the nearest town was only three miles away.

The second report changed all these facts. This report stated that the young man, who was drunk, had crossed the white center line and crashed into a lumber truck traveling in the eastbound lane. My client didn't want to pursue a lawsuit but only wanted to know how her son had died, for, as she tearfully told me, he had never taken a drink in his life. She begged me to find the truth about her son's death.

So, I traveled to Grants to talk with the state police who, along with the justices of the peace, were the only law in many small towns throughout New Mexico at that time. I was told to look for Nash Garcia, the local state patrolman.

I finally found Garcia strolling down the main street of Grants with two attractive young women, one on each arm. A third woman yelled at him from a second-story window of the Navajo Inn.

Garcia talked with me while expertly juggling four 38-caliber bullets, and told me that while yes, he had signed the two accident reports, no, he never went to the scene of the accident.

"Hell no," he said, "I was up at Thoreau playing poker, and I wouldn't go down to that *malpais* [literally "bad ground"], where them damn rattlesnakes are six feet long! Bud Rice makes out all my reports and if you call me as a witness, I'll swear that the boy was dead drunk, and I'll have the whiskey bottle half full to prove it. Why don't you go back to Colorado, where you belong?" (And welcome to New Mexico.)

The "Robber of '66"

I wasn't about to give up on this one—After tracking down Justice of the Peace Howard Neal ("Bud") Rice, and investigating the case a little further, I decided that the well-known nickname for this particular justice of the peace—"The Robber of '66"—was right on the money.

Bud Rice owned and operated a combination trading post, gas station, garage, and towing business in Cubero, along old Highway 66 about 20 miles east of Grants and 46 miles west of Albuquerque. Because of his reputation along this particular stretch of Highway 66, the small community surrounding Bud's house and businesses became known as "Budville." Rice made sure he kept in good standing with the state police, and each Christmas gave each member of the force a bottle of good liquor and a carton of cigarettes. Bud also threw a big barbeque for his law enforcement friends each 4th of July.

He was once convicted of assault, but thanks to friends in high places, he received a suspended sentence and was eventually pardoned by the Governor in 1942.

From the late 1940s into the 1950s, Rice served as the local justice of the peace in Budville. And, while he was not a trained lawyer, he did effectively represent his friends before the magistrate judge in nearby Grants. While he was known to help needy children and would help bail his neighbors out of jail, many more people came to dislike and distrust him due to his monopoly in the area. As the owner of the only wrecker on that open stretch of Highway 66 between the Rio Puerco, west of Albuquerque, and Grants, he became notorious not only for charging high towing prices but also for demanding ridiculously high prices for repairs. In one often-repeated story, Rice once towed a stranger's car to Budville and replaced the vehicle's fan belt. When the car owner heard the high price of the newly installed fan belt, he objected vehemently. Bud Rice took out a pocketknife and slit the new belt. The he ordered the aghast traveler to get that car off his property. He also had a favorite trick of charging exorbitantly high prices for tire snow chains after telling travelers they would need chains west of Gallup, where, as he always told them, the weather was bound to be rough.

As a justice of the peace, Rice set new record highs for fines, and was particularly hard on out-of-town speeders, who often faced fines higher than $60 a ticket (about $380 today)—an exorbitant amount in the 1950s and 1960s. Bud also enraged other area tow companies by declaring that any wrecks west of the Rio Puerco River and all the way to Grants belonged to him alone. After all, he said, the other tow companies were welcome to all wrecks in the short stretch from the western edge of Albuquerque to the Rio Puerco River.

But back to my client's son. After the accident, the young man's car had been towed to Rice's store and service station in Budville.

Since Rice often appropriated any unclaimed property, in this case he claimed the young man's car. When I got back to Denver, I was able to reassure my client that her son was never drunk but unfortunately had been injured along one of the wilder stretches of Highway 66, far from medical help but close to Budville. The tiny lady was relieved that her son's name was cleared.

The rest of the story

On November 18, 1967, the regime in and around Budville came to an abrupt and shocking end when Rice and one of his employees, Blanche Brown, an 82-year-old retired schoolteacher, were gunned down in cold blood at his gas station. A customer had stopped to buy gas and a few items in the store. Bud went outside to pump two dollars worth of gas. When Rice went back inside after pumping the gas, he found the customer and Blanche arguing over the bill. The situation escalated, and both Blanche and Bud were shot dead. Bud's wife Flossie was tied up, $450 was taken out of the till, and all the lights were turned out. The customer fled. Unbeknownst to the killer, another witness survived to tell the story. A housekeeper, hiding in a nearby room, saw it all, and untied Flossie once the man was gone. Though they called the police immediately, it took nearly a year to find the killer and bring him to justice.

In another twist in the story, State Policeman Nash Garcia was also murdered, and his car "torched" by two Navajo men. On Friday, April 11, 1952, two brothers intentionally broke several traffic laws in order to get Garcia to chase them in his patrol car. They lured him onto the Navajo reservation, and shot him as his car went around a bend in a mountainous area. They dragged him from his car and beat him to death with a rifle butt. They then burned his body in his car.

The brothers were found guilty of first-degree murder in Federal Judge Carl A. Hatch's court in Albuquerque, and the jury determined they should get the death penalty. Judge Hatch changed the sentence to life imprisonment because of the mental status of both defendants. They were sent to the U.S. Medical Center for Prisoners in Springfield, Missouri, for the rest of their natural lives. I assume they are still there.

3
Our New World

When we left metropolitan Denver in June 1947, we arrived at a much smaller and very different place. We had sold our beautiful, brand-new and modern home on busy Wadsworth Avenue in west Denver, to move into our new home in Albuquerque. For a short while our new home was a traditional pueblo-style flat-roofed adobe home on narrow and meandering Guadalupe Trail. Our new neighbors were friendly, including our next-door neighbor who had 22 children; they explained that they would have had 23, "but one of the twins died."

**Bob and the kids shortly after we moved from Denver.
Bob made the chaps the two younger children are wearing.**

A 1950s postcard shows the heart of Albuquerque, at the corner of
Fourth and Central, looking east.

Downtown Albuquerque, 1950s, looking east toward the Sandia Mountains.
The east and west mesas were vacant. (Photo by Eldred R. Harrington,
courtesy of the Center for Southwest Research, University of New Mexico)

In 1947, Albuquerque was a small, unique, and intriguing place to
live and work. The population was close to 97,000, swelled by former military men who had served at the two local military bases, Sandia Base and

Kirtland Air Force Base, during World War II. Many had learned to love the big skies, big scenery, and abundant sunshine and moved their families to the Southwest. People came from all parts of the U.S. and the world—some were on their way to California when they ran out of money or their cars broke down on Route 66 west of town. Many were looking for new lives and new careers.

The week we arrived, the *Albuquerque Journal* was filled with political ads for candidates I would come to know very well in the years ahead. Johnny Flaska, who was a well-known wrestling coach, wanted your vote for him as County Sheriff; Thomas Mabry was running for the Governor's job. Clinton P. Anderson was running for the U.S. Senate seat he would go on to win and hold for many years. Democratic Senator Dionisio (Dennis) Chavez was also prominently featured in the news.

Dennis Chavez (third from the left), was a criminal lawyer who served as U.S. Senator for New Mexico from 1935 to 1962. Here he gathers with a group of western senators, including New Mexico Senator Carl A. Hatch, second from left. The group had just left the White House after urging President Roosevelt to allocate funds for reclamation of irrigation projects in their western states. (Photo dated July 2, 1935, courtesy of the Library of Congress)

A glance at the *Journal* showed headlines that included a mix of local and national news:

Floods on the Columbia River
$3,686,733,250 Received for Navy Appropriations
New Well at Conservancy Beach
Airliner Crash near Gallup; 30 Persons Safe
Warning: Bubonic Plague
University Rejects 25 Polish Boys No Scholarships—Lack of Funds
622 Graduate at Albuquerque High School

Jimmy Demaret was leading the Albuquerque Open at the Albuquerque Country Club. He won on Sunday with a score of 268 (20 under par) and took home the $10,000 first prize.

General Electric stock was quoted at 41 ¾, General Cigar at 23, and General Motors at 9.

Advertisements included familiar products and items expected of a fair-sized post-war metropolitan area. Belz Furniture advertized a solid oak living room set for $139. Montgomery Wards would sell you a 93-piece china set for $27.88. Hinkels Department Store sold cotton "Organdia" dresses for $14.95. Fair Stores had work shoes for $3.92. Rubbing alcohol was seven cents a pint at Payless Drugs. Allstate tires were $14.95 apiece at Sears. Walgreens sold five-cent candy or three pieces for 10 cents. Walgreens also had Tide (a brand-new product) for 29 cents a box—the same price as Duz Detergent at Payless.

Monarch Airlines advertised trips to Grand Junction, Colorado, for $23.30 (noting that the trip was scheduled to take 3 2/3 hours) and to Salt Lake City for $32.05 (that trip took six hours).

A six-room "modern house" was $9,500. The agency asked you to call 2-4893 for particulars.

Down at the KIMO Theatre on Central Avenue, Jennifer Jones, Gregory Peck, and Joseph Cotton starred in "Duel in the Sun." The CHIEF Theater was running "The Bishop's Wife," with Cary Grant, Loretta Young, and David Niven.

The modern-day KIMO Theatre, restored to better-than-new, still at its original site on Central Avenue.

Would this be a good place to live? Would we miss Denver too much? We would soon see!

Highs and lows of the law

While I eventually found Albuquerque to be a great place to live and work, my first impression was that as a woman attorney I was not going to be taken seriously. There were two other women attorneys in Albuquerque at that time, neither of whom had a very high profile nor was very active at the Bar. For example, one of these attorneys had written a 20-page will for a transient client who didn't really have enough property to justify a two-page will. To add insult to injury, she then circulated the will around among the male attorneys, asking their comments about whether or not it was an appropriately written will! And, several years later I had to laugh when the local newspapers reported a case in which another woman lawyer and I were opponents. The story was front-page news and portrayed our case as a sort of hen party, giving little attention to the facts in the actual case itself.

I didn't encounter outright, overt discrimination as much as I found condescension from the male lawyers in Albuquerque. In addition, when I first arrived I did find that legal business in New Mexico was pretty well channeled into a just a few local firms. Albuquerque had two principal banks, the First National Bank and Albuquerque National Bank. All of Albuquerque National Bank's business was handled by the Simms law firm. The other national bank was the province of the Rodey law firm. Any matters involving the Santa Fe Railway belonged to the Johnson firm. The various other pieces of legal business were apportioned out among the smaller firms and the sole practitioners, including me.

I have to add, however, that in what would seem to be a hostile environment, I made some very good friends. In the early days I received a great deal of help from many of the older attorneys in the area, most notably Judge John F. Simms Sr., who headed up the Simms firm.

John Simms, Sr., headed one of the two largest firms in Albuquerque and would become a trusted friend and mentor.
(Photo courtesy of the Simms firm)

At that time the Simms firm had 13 attorneys. Even with that number of attorneys on hand, Judge Simms told me he still had to work very hard. He reluctantly closed the office on Saturdays so the firm's secretaries could have time with their families. He also confided that although it was true there were 13 attorneys sitting around his office or whose feet he said he "had to trip over each day," he still did much of the work himself—even down to examining abstracts, a job traditionally done by beginning attorneys in a firm.

I tried very hard to maintain a standard of excellence, and I received many guardianship matters, small cases that required a lot of legwork, and cases that were inconsistent with the Simms firm's program. In other words, I was the person to go to when the case didn't fit the usual mix of that firm's cases. It took a while to be taken seriously by the state bench and Bar, but I didn't ask any special consideration because of being female, and I didn't give any. Instead, I really tried to be a "gentleman" in matters legal. One of my brothers at the Bar once asked, 'How can you be so nice outside the court, but when you come into court you tear our guts out?" My rejoinder always was that I was an advocate, and my services were for hire in proper cases and that I wanted to be taken as an attorney, not as a *female* attorney. My credo, long before discrimination against women came into the spotlight, was the same advice I offered to all my female and black and minority friends. This was, just do twice as much work, at first (but not forever), even for half as much pay, and eventually you'll make it fine.

My first office in Albuquerque

My first law office in Albuquerque was in a storefront off North Fourth Street, behind Keith's Drug Store and next door to the office of an elderly general practitioner, Dr. Gore. The neighborhood storefront office was the scene for many legal adventures, some with a few extra legal stripes, I would say.

Early one morning, soon after I opened the office, about 25 Hispanic people crowded into the outer room. The leader of the throng was a tall, red-headed man with a long red beard, by the name of Zamora, and Zamora was a very angry man. Everyone was speaking at once, rapidly and all in Spanish, which I didn't understand. We found chairs for a few of the group and the rest leaned against the walls.

The group's complaint involved a school bus problem, and the parents had every reason to be angry. All the members of the group lived in the north end of Albuquerque, east of the railroad tracks. Their children's grade school was Lew Wallace School, located on the *west* side of the tracks. The State Board of Education had issued an edict that no school bus could cross the railroad tracks, and so these people's children had to be bused from their homes, down to the heart of town, under the Santa Fe Railway Overpass, and then placed in another school bus, which then delivered them to the other side of the railroad tracks and on to school. The children had to board the first bus by seven am, when it was cold and dark in the winter, and the reverse trip got them home later at night.

We organized this group by selecting three of the leaders, headed by the redheaded and red-bearded Mr. Zamora, and got on the agenda for the next School Board meeting. The Board heard the families' grievances and resolved them, and as a result many of these people became loyal clients for many years afterward.

Prejudice against working women, particularly women lawyers, was all around. This wasn't personal, just a sign of the times, and persisted no matter what license or certification a woman had.

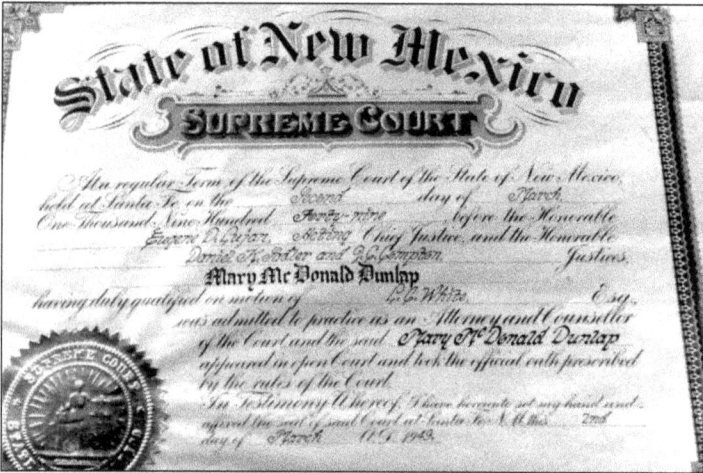

My official license to practice law in New Mexico, issued in 1949.

Women were supposed to be in the home, not in the courthouse. I was once told by an elderly gentleman who wanted his will drawn that I couldn't possibly be a real lawyer because, as he said, "Real lawyers don't have calluses on their hands." Another prospective client told me I couldn't be a real lawyer because I drove a pickup truck, and he loudly declared to anyone who might be listening, "Everybody knows that lawyers don't drive pickups."

On the plus side, in addition to help from some senior attorneys, I also received help and had cases referred to me from several justices of the peace, who could rely on me to come in on short notice. One of my favorites was Justice of the Peace Tom Padilla, whose office was located on North Fourth Street. My first case in his court was a real eye-opener and a good introduction to the way the law really worked in New Mexico. The case involved an eviction action. My client had purchased a corner lot, and planned to build a hardware store there. The lot held six small cabin-like apartments, and we had been able to help move people from five of the six out to other inexpensive housing areas, leaving only one, which was holding up the works.

The last residents refused to move. So, we filed an eviction action. The case fell in Judge Padilla's court because the land was in his precinct. When my client and I drove up to the address we had been given for Judge Padilla's court, we saw a sign for a welding and well-drilling shop. We were waved inside and told that this was indeed Judge Padilla's court.

Then Judge Padilla stomped in, clad in muddy coveralls and boots. He peeled off the coveralls in the middle of the room, revealing his matted work clothes underneath. He strolled over to his desk, pulled out an electric razor and shaved while asking, "What case is this and what's it all about?" After we got everything underway, and after a lot of effort and time, the last cabin was vacated and construction could begin.

Over time I found that Judge Padilla always had a hot pot of coffee waiting for the lawyers on his woodstove in the back room of the welding shop. We all sat around on nail kegs and oil drums, and nearly always were served mutton stew before court opened. The stew was delicious. When he retired, and the highway department bought his property, Judge Padilla gave me his old cast iron wood stove, and I cherish it still. The coal-black stove has made a perfect planter for bright red geraniums for many years.

Although Judge Padilla was not a lawyer, in his court he reached results that were generally fair and always arrived at honestly. He also was a great storyteller, and especially kind to young and green attorneys like me, who always needed all the help we could get.

In New Mexico, the justices of the peace were often the only judges available because the district judges 'rode the circuit,' and generally had to cover several counties within their district. The individual justice of the peace and the state policemen stationed in the area were really the main law enforcement officers at that time. I had learned about this system first-hand when I met Bud Rice and Officer Nash Garcia during my first visit to New Mexico.

Unfortunately, unlike the case of Tom Padilla's court, many abuses arose out of the justice of the peace system. As a result, the Albuquerque bench and Bar began its efforts to put into place a Small Claims Court system in metropolitan areas with large enough populations. I later was appointed as one of the first judges of the Small Claims Court in Albuquerque. The Bernalillo County Small Claims Court was established in an effort to filter off some of the legal business of the justices of the peace and to handle some matters locally, to relieve the pressure on the District Court. Magistrates followed further down the line. The Small Claims Court usually handled claims under $7,000. In this court the plaintiff often represented himself, although lawyers were also allowed in most cases.

During this time I served as a member of the Albuquerque Bar Association Civil Rights Committee, a group that met regularly to discuss complaints. Unfortunately, many were complaints of police brutality. The Civil Rights Committee was an advisory group only, and had no authority; however, we occasionally rattled the cages of police departments and others. I was a sort of "water boy" for the team on this committee but I was not unhappy about this because, after all, at least I was on the team. Whatever took legwork and investigation was my beat. If a restaurant refused to serve a black patron except in a brown carry-out bag, and out the back door, I interviewed the party and brought back the reports. In every city police brutality charge, the chief and his officer involved came to our hearing and uniformly denied that any such event ever occurred. That is, all except one case that I recall very well.

A high school student and his father, who was blind, had a home on South Second Street, near the city dump. The area was frequented by thieves, who often dumped their unwanted loot in the area. On one occasion, the city police discovered some costume jewelry that had been reported stolen, and took the young student in for questioning. He was seated by a bank of steel filing cabinets. When questioned about the jewelry, he answered that he knew nothing about it. The officers didn't like his answers and so they threw him against the filing cabinets again and again, rupturing his eardrum, fracturing his ribs, and bruising him severely.

I had medical photographs taken of the bruises, and a medical report showed the injuries were consistent with being thrown against the cabinets. However, despite the fact that the abuse was evident and the police department admitted it, in the end, the boy's family didn't want to take any action because several family members were city employees and feared losing their jobs.

During this period I did a great deal of pro-bono work, and in the long run it was beneficial to me. I secured the first charter and incorporated the Registered Nurses Association in New Mexico. I also incorporated the Licensed Practical Nurses working in the state of New Mexico. When non-profit organizations could get nowhere or when it seemed that officials were standing still and nothing was going forward, I helped the nonprofits incorporate and got them a grant to help them operate. During this time, also, I got myself into *Who's Who of American Women*, was the charter president of Zonta, a service club for professional women, and was written up in a book called *Women Lawyers in the United States*, by Dorothy Thomas. I also was an active guest speaker at many women's clubs, such as the Navajo Club.

Albuquerque people

Thinking back, I realize that it was a marvelous time to practice law. The membership of the Bar was small and, in most cases, our contacts were informal. We conducted much of our business over the telephone and it never occurred to us that one day we would have to put everything in writing to protect ourselves from our fellow attorneys.

It was the custom of many of the members of the Bar to meet at Magidson's Restaurant on Central Avenue, to enjoy both the fellowship of our fellow attorneys and some of the best hot pastrami sandwiches and chicken broth with kreplach around. Papa Magidson's dill pickles were delicious. At the Court Café, down the street from the Bernalillo County Courthouse, many matters were discussed and some settled over tasty meals. It was a different day, and my children were welcomed even in the bar area, where the bartender always made them a special drink they named the "Horse's Neck." It was a sort of Albuquerque-style Shirley Temple.

Some local leaders

There was then, as now, really only one federal judicial court, then presided over by Judge Carl A. Hatch (much more about Judge Hatch later). He was, of course, a former U.S. Senator and the author of the Hatch Act. The seven senior members of the Bar were Judge Hatch, Judge Sam Bratton, Judge Kiker, Hugh Woodward, Governor Hannett, John Simms, Sr. of the Simms firm, and Pearce Rodey, head of the Rodey firm.

We had only three judges in the State District Court, and our Municipal Court was presided over by Judge Harry Robins, a very colorful figure. I recall representing an American Indian who had been arrested for urinating in a public park.

We went to court. Judge Robins said, as he dismissed the case, "Hell, if I put every Indian in jail who pissed in a park, I'd either have to build a huge new jail or else turn out everybody I've got in there right now."

This was also the era of Senator Dennis Chavez, who was a self-made man. He was in touch with his people in New Mexico and was available to them at all times. His aides were always able to help anyone who came to his office.

We also had Sheriff Johnny Flaska, a former professional athlete who was the consummate sheriff: He never missed a christening, a marriage, a funeral, or a wake, and was always a welcome sight at all these events.

This was also the time of former New Mexico Governor (1935–1938) and then Albuquerque Mayor Clyde Tingley, who added a new word to the English language—"chowse." Most people pronounce this as "chaos," but in deference to Governor Tingley, we lawyers all started saying "chowse." Mayor Tingley had great plans for Albuquerque, many of which really made the city a better place to live. (An entertaining and in-depth book on Mayor and Carrie Tingley's life is *Clyde Tingley's New Deal for New Mexico, 1935–1938*, by Albuquerque author Lucinda Lucero Sachs.)

Albuquerque Mayor Clyde Tingley.

Those responsible for developing much of the Northeast Heights included Dale Bellamah, Sam Hoffman, Fred Mossman, and Ed Snow. Their major developments include Hoffmantown, Snow Heights, Mesa Village, Princess Jeanne, Bellehaven, the Kirtland Addition and earlier subdivisions east of Carlisle Avenue. Harvey Golightly, better known as Colonel Golightly, built the Bel-Air subdivision, bounded by Carlisle, San Mateo, Menaul and Candelaria Road, before FHA requirements. The houses sold quickly and the community was unique because it had its own water tank. It was annexed into the city in 1951.

At one memorable city commission meeting, with Mayor Tingley presiding, a proposed subdivision was being reviewed for approval. This was to be the first of many subdivisions built by Dale Bellamah, one of America's first large-scale home builders. This particular development was designed to provide homes for World War II veterans. Some protestors pointed out that the main street of the subdivision would be directly in the path of the Embudo Arroyo, which regularly carried the runoff from the Sandia Mountains across town to the Rio Grande River on the west. Like so many dry arroyos in the Southwest, a good rain produced a torrent, and the arroyo always spilled over into anything in its path. Nearly every August, Second and Fourth streets were seriously flooded at least once. It was nearly like clockwork each summer.

Mayor Tingley told the protestors, "I could drink in a teacup all the water that will ever run down that arroyo."

Dale Bellamah built the subdivision, and it is reputed that the curbs, which were 12 inches high in the blueprints, ended up being only six inches high. And, like clockwork, during the annual runoff of the Embudo Arroyo, the water raced down, out of its immense teacup, knocking down six-foot walls, running through the living rooms and out the patio doors of many houses. Many homes were demolished.

Street characters

The town was also small enough that we were able to enjoy visits from a number of local characters we saw on the streets every day. Many of these street people also regularly made the rounds of our law offices. Others had regular spots near the County Courthouse, such as the blind Indian woman who sold gum. Her family would drop her off early in the morning and she would gently call out "Chicle, chicle" as she sat by the curb selling gum all day, until someone came to pick her up in the afternoon.

One unforgettable character was a tall black woman, at least 85 years old, who came to all our offices asking for funds to help the members of her church convert the pastor's residence into a formal church. She was over six feet tall, always dressed all in white, and walked many, many miles to make her daily rounds. She carried a rolled-up paper scroll, which was her "roll of honor." If you gave a small donation to her worthy cause, your name would appear on the roll. She always had an interesting story to tell, and the latest gossip, and her visit was always worth a donation, whether or not the money was ever actually channeled into changing the residence into a church. This we'll never know.

Once I asked her how she could see so well at her age without glasses. She told me that she had worn glasses for many years, and then the Lord had mysteriously "quickened" her eyesight, so she threw her glasses away. One day her granddaughter asked her, "Granny, where are your glasses?" She replied, "Sister, where's your faith?"

Another person who regularly made the rounds of the offices was known only as "Jim." He was about five feet tall, wore a greasy little cap, and always needed 50 cents to buy coffee. He said he had been on Welfare for many years, his wife couldn't work, and he himself wasn't able to work. He said the money afforded him by the Welfare Department allowed him to eke out a miserable existence, but he never had enough money to buy a pound of coffee and hadn't had coffee for years.

Well, all of us who admire the Columbian mocha bean—perhaps to the detriment of our health—were always open to giving Jim 50 cents, and he went off merrily on his way. I assume he might have bought a cup or two of coffee, but it's more probable that he bought a bottle of Garden Deluxe wine.

For several years, a tall Navajo also made the office rounds, seeking funds "to bury his dead wife." He said he came from the community of Cañon, and his wife had just died. He claimed he didn't have the money to buy the sacred corn meal, and the other accouterments required for an appropriate Indian burial. In addition to being drunk most of the time, he seemed to have a poor memory—or else a multitude of wives had departed his life.

A former municipal judge, once a sparkling, witty member of the Bar, and a popular judge, also joined the street crowd after an unfortunate visit to the State Hospital in Las Vegas. Police Judge Elgan C. Gober, who had reportedly been stripped of all his funds by a former wife, had been committed to the State Hospital for a prefrontal lobotomy—at his wife's request. In reality, he hadn't lost his memory—merely his reasoning ability. Once he was released from the hospital, he cadged drinks, picking up spare pop bottles to earn a little money. From time to time we'd invite him to have coffee with us, feeling great sadness and pity for the formerly lively and intelligent judge, now reduced to a spare, gray shadow that drifted up and down Central Avenue. (The physician who invented the prefrontal lobotomy was awarded the Nobel Prize in 1949, the same year we arrived in Albuquerque.)

Mrs. Blumberg's will

Early in October 1950, I went out to the Nazareth Sanitarium to draw a will for an elderly widow who had come to New Mexico because she was a friend of the medical director of the hospital. The Dominican Sisters of Grand Rapids, Michigan, built the three-story, red-tile-roofed Sanitarium with several airy courtyards in 1930 for patients with tuberculosis. The Sanitarium had 40 to 50 beds, and was in a desolate location more than 10 miles by dirt road from Albuquerque, in an area generally known as the "Rattlesnake Mesa." Corrales was reached by a single-lane steel bridge back then. (The original Nazareth Sanitarium building was torn down in 1973.)

I took copious notes and talked with Mrs. Blumberg about her property and her beneficiaries. Her estate would be extensive—all blue chip stocks, bonds, municipals, and lots of real estate. The targets of her benevolence were all East Coast charitable and educational organizations. For example, a large bequest was to go the Boston Lying-in Hospital.

Before Mrs. Blumberg's will was ready, on October 20, 1950, my daughter Elizabeth Jean was born. Within a short time, I returned to complete the matter of the will. Mrs. Blumberg insisted that we amend the will to give the new baby $2,500. She stated that she had done business with lawyers all her life but never had one stop her business in the midst of everything to be delivered of a child. In her words, she found this "absolutely enchanting."

I promptly declined, despite her protests, and finally told her that if I did this kind of thing I would certainly be disbarred.

It was not only my code of ethics that deterred me but the results of my mother's strict standards of honesty that were impressed upon us all throughout the years. For example, my stepfather once borrowed $2,500 from a friend to outfit his new barbershop in our small hometown of Eureka. After my stepfather failed to repay the loan, my mother worked for one family, who had paid the loan, for nearly 20 years. She repaid the money, with interest. Monday morning found her doing the family's laundry; on Tuesday she did their ironing, and on Saturday cleaned their three-story house top to bottom.

I once took a doll dress from a friend without her permission, and my mother turned that dress into an albatross for me that rivaled that of the Ancient Mariner's. Code of ethics be damned, my mother kept me straight in this matter, as in many matters throughout my life. I never had any trouble determining what was my money and what belonged to others that I was holding in trust.

I've never believed the study and practice of law bestows upon a man or woman any special qualities, but only refines and sharpens those that he or she brings to the study of law and to the profession. I decry the intellectual dishonesty of my brethren in the abstract almost as much as their stealing money from clients, to whom they owe the highest duty of honesty and competence.

4

BEGINNINGS

A common question that I have learned to field and answer, depending upon who asks, is "Why did you ever become a lawyer?"

The real reason I became a lawyer is that my grandfather, John James Leonal Kramm, wanted me to be a lawyer and to work for the Santa Fe Railroad. In his mind, working for the Santa Fe Railway was the ultimate career. This may have had something to do with his many friends and associates in Manchester, Kansas, in Dickinson County, where he and my grandmother, Mary Arminta Leech Kramm, owned and operated the Manchester Hotel.

My grandparents and their young children. Left to right: Grandmother Mary Arminta Kramm, baby Earl, Roy, Grandpa Leo Kramm, and my mother, Faye Violet. Another son, Francis, would be born later.

Our family gathers in front of the Manchester Hotel, in Manchester, Kansas, in 1916. I am the baby in the photo, here sitting on my grandfather's lap. My mother, Faye Violet Kramm McDonald, is the tall woman 6th from the right, and my grandmother and namesake Mary Arminta Kramm is to the left, standing right behind my grandfather.

In 1887, the Atchison, Topeka and Santa Fe Railway built a branch line from Neva (three miles west of Strong City, Kansas) through Manchester to Superior, Nebraska. The Santa Fe Railway had a station in Manchester and railroad workers and travelers were a major source of revenue for my grandparents' hotel. My two uncles, Roy and Francis Kramm, had long careers as conductors with the Santa Fe Railway, and my father, Isaac McDonald, was a station agent.

Although my grandfather's dream was that I become a Santa Fe Railway lawyer, I had to disappoint him. I found out very early after arriving in Albuquerque that the Santa Fe Railroad was very well represented by Bryan Johnson and his firm, and they did not particularly need my services.

I had much help and many factors helped me go to college and on to law school. From the very beginning, scholarship was always easy for me.

When I entered the University of Kansas in 1935, I had two jobs, a resident scholarship, which provided room and board in a women's scholarship hall, and $35, and there was my beginning.

My family was extremely poor, and my mother, Faye Violet Kramm McDonald Putnam, struggled to raise me and my stepbrother John, and my sisters Twila Mae and Donna Marie Putnam, who were born many years after me. My mother's parents had never approved of her marriage to my father, and in effect had told her that she 'had made her bed, so now go lie in it.' Pretty quickly after I was born, my mother was on her own in the world.

My mother had pretty bad luck with her choice of husbands, perhaps proving that opposites do attract. She was the most honest, ethical, and hard-working person you could ever meet, and managed to find humor even in the worst of circumstances. She also was a very strong Lutheran. My father vanished soon after I was born, and we heard nothing from him until the night I was graduating from Eureka High School.

My mother's second husband, John Putnam, was a handsome and charismatic man, who had a small son and ran a barbershop in the Greenwood Hotel in Eureka, Kansas. My mother was concerned about John's son Johnny, who was seldom in school. This was, after all, in the midst of the Great Depression, and Johnny and his father often nearly lived off the land. For example, the two would go rabbit hunting in the winter, and the spoils were then hung on a clothesline, sort of an unsightly but effective outdoor freezer. Years later Faye admitted that one reason she had married Johnny's father was to give the child a good home. Once in school, Johnny became a good student and went on to become a teacher and school administrator in Kansas. My stepfather had a serious dislike of me all his life, and had a real temper, which only grew worse with time.

Many years later my stepfather was hospitalized in the Osawatomie (Kansas) Psychiatric Hospital after a violent fight, which may have led to a stroke. He remained in the psychiatric hospital for the rest of his life, except for one brief and scary escape. We had no telephone, so there was no way for the hospital to warn us that he had escaped. We saw him coming up the street, but luckily he was intercepted by the police before he could reach our little house and carry out his threat to murder my mother and us all. Through all this, and throughout her long life, my mother persisted, trusting in her Lutheran faith, and facing most barriers with great good humor.

We were all affected by the Depression in spite of several oil booms in Kansas. To say that we were poor, particularly during the early days after my father left, is an understatement. My mother never dwelt on self-pity, but abruptly started cooking and taking in washing and cleaning houses to support the family.

Despite our lack of money, Eureka was a good place to grow up. As far as schools, churches, and a good town library, we could count ourselves as wealthy. Our Andrew Carnegie Library, part of the nationwide legacy of the Carnegie fortune, was a haven for me as well as many of our friends.

The Andrew Carnegie Library in Eureka was a haven for me and many others. The Library recently was completely restored.

I loved school, and knowledge seemed to come easy to me. My mother had only an eighth grade education and was always proud of me and encouraged me to do my best. To me, getting more education was the only key I had to a better life.

Even though Eureka was small (in 1933 the population was 4,178), we had nearly everything a larger town could offer. We could swim and fish in the Fall River all summer, and at Eureka High we had a school newspaper, dances, a great debate team, clubs, picnics, and anything you could think of. Our senior class put on a terrific senior play, and we had all sorts of events, even an annual watermelon-eating contest.

And, later, Eureka became known for Utopia College, founded by wealthy financier Roger Babson. Babson selected Eureka as the site for his Utopia College shortly after World War II. He selected Eureka because of its distance from probable targets should a nuclear war occur. His intention was to develop an underground college campus that would be safe from nuclear attack. At that time it was said that Eureka was the exact center of the U.S. He also believed that central Kansas would have the natural resources, such as oil, minerals and grain, needed to rebuild following a nuclear war. Although Utopia College never moved underground or grew very large, the two-year college continued until 1969 as the Midwest Institute.

For a small town, Eureka had lots to offer. The watermelon fest was a treat for all of us; this photo was taken in the early 1930s. I am third from the right, next to my stepfather John Putnam. My mother Faye is at the far left.

Eureka was small enough that you knew everyone in town and of course they knew you and watched out for you, too. This could be a good thing and a not-so-good thing, as I found out with the Good Reverend (more about him later).

I also had help from friends and early mentors. One was old Judge Wicker, who thought my analytical mind and easy scholarship would tend to make it possible for me to become a lawyer. The Judge also impressed upon me that everyone had the right to be represented in court, even the worst defendant imaginable. It wasn't a matter of worldly goods, either—the law really was sacred and stood apart. Judge Wicker always carried a briefcase, which always seemed oddly lightweight. Once I asked him what he had in that briefcase, and he opened it to show me a starched white shirt. Seeing my puzzled look, he smiled and added that it was very useful at all times for a lawyer to be able to leave town in a hurry. Judge Wicker also gave me a large stuffed barn owl with its wings extended. He told me that this had been in his office for many years, and he wanted me to have it as I went off to college. The owl never made it to the campus; instead, I donated it to the Eureka High School Library, where it may or may not still be gracing an upper shelf.

I really grew up in my grandfather's hotel lobby in the Manchester Hotel and in my stepfather's barbershop in the Greenwood Hotel, at 310 Main Street in Eureka. The Greenwood Hotel was the most impressive building in town, and the center for many oil and cattle deals, as well as weddings, dances and big band concerts, not to mention lots of political action.

The Greenwood Hotel was the social and business center for Greenwood County. The old hotel, first opened in October 1883, was restored in 2012. It was said that more than $1 billion worth of cattle was traded in its lobby.

The barbershop was a sort of poor man's social club, and as a result I have to say I have truly never known a stranger in my life. The barbershop was on the ground floor of the hotel and I worked there as soon as I was able, cleaning the floors and even emptying the spittoons.

However, despite all our encounters with the hard realities of life, I still brought to the practice of law an amazing naiveté or, as my mother more aptly put it, I was "as green as a gourd." Thanks to my mother and my grandfather, I developed a very strict moral code.

My great-grandfather Mattias Kramm and great-grandmother Maria Magdalina Sohuetz Kramm. Mattias, who homesteaded at Vine Creek, Kansas, was born in Niederbrecken, Germany, in 1820; he died at Vine Creek in 1889. Maria, born in Eppstein, Germany, in 1836, died in Manchester, Kansas, in 1910.

My great-grandfather, Matthias Kramm, was an original Kansas homesteader whose farm was near Vine Creek in western Kansas. The rule was that you could own 640 acres if you proved that you had established a farm and regularly tilled the land. A longtime family story is that when great-grandfather Kramm fell seriously ill, and his homestead was in danger of being taken away, his neighbors saved his farm by chipping in and plowing the fields for him.

I'd always worked with the public, even with some very tough types, but most people were very protective of me. For example, when I was 13 I worked in a hamburger joint in Eureka and closed it late every night, carrying home with me the day's receipts, a piece of lead pipe, and a loaded .38 revolver. The restaurant was in a tough neighborhood but luckily my good friend at the time was the town bootlegger, who would not allow any rough or crude talk when I was around. Occasionally he had to throw somebody out of the place when they got a little too unruly.

If you look back at the history of little towns throughout Kansas, you'll see that nearly every town, no matter how tiny, seemed to have at least two things—a church and a school. School was a special haven for me. In our little town of Eureka, I received what was then called a classical education, with Latin classes and an emphasis on English literature. Luckily I was also asked to join the debate team in high school and my experience in debate helped me tremendously in later life, particularly in extemporaneous speaking. I found I loved speaking in public and never had trouble standing up and speaking in any situation. As a result, if any presentation had to be made, my classmates looked to me to do it. I became President of the Student Council and a member of the National Honor Society.

Our Eureka High School Student Council; I'm in the front row, second from the right.

I was fortunate to be chosen as Valedictorian of our senior class, and to receive a full scholarship, with tuition and board and room to the University of Kansas in Lawrence. This included housing in a residence hall for the four years of my undergraduate study.

Some of my most treasured friends, who have remained friends all our lives, included the three Harrys: handsome Harry Anderson, gentle and kind Harry Paulson, and brainy Harry Hannibal Hollowell. Harry Anderson became a rancher in Greenwood County; Harry Paulson, whose family owned the Paulson Shoe Store on Main Street, remained in Eureka to care for his aged mother and married only after she had passed away. Harry Hollowell was a top student, and incidentally the only black student at Eureka High. He was selected as Salutatorian, but on graduation night, as we all assembled to march into the auditorium, it was announced that Harry would not be allowed to march with us. The Powers That Be announced that Harry Hollowell could march in to the ceremony only after all we white students did. I was outraged and bellowed, "If Harry doesn't march, none of us will march!" It was a real standoff, but we won, and Harry and I marched in, arm and arm, to graduate. Harry went on to become a well-known and respected lawyer.

As I mentioned earlier, my long-lost father also showed up on graduation night and proclaimed, "Minta Mary, now I want to be a father to you." I don't know where it came from, but I said, "Buster, you're just eighteen years too late." He slunk out of town a second time, and we never heard from him again.

I had help from many people in Eureka. The kind people there wanted me to succeed. Ward McGinnis, a cattleman and oilman and head of the one of the families who helped me the most, also acted as a moral compass. Like the old judge before, Ward told me that once I became a lawyer, I should never turn down anyone who needed help, and the matter of the fee would take care of itself. This advice has proved to be pretty nearly correct. I have turned few people down. If a person had a cause, I have tried to espouse it if I thought it was proper and legal. If there was anything to be done to help someone, I usually have tried to do it. Ward McGinnis's wife Harriett and her friends helped me immeasurably when they organized a clothing drive and collected new clothing so I would have clothing for school. The townspeople and my mother also helped me immeasurably with my oldest son Sheldon Lee, after an impulsive marriage quickly failed. My mother took care of Sheldon while I went on to school. It was not an easy decision but I knew that education and an eventual law degree were my best hopes.

My future husband, Robert A. (Bob) Dunlap, strikes a pose with a close "friend" at the University of Kansas.

At the University of Kansas, in Lawrence, I was lucky enough to find all sorts of jobs, including some cleaning and waitressing jobs. We truly were children of the Great Depression, and were always happy to find work, and somehow made our way. My future husband Robert also struggled, and by some miracle was able to talk someone into letting him live on campus in the student hospital. In the summer he worked on farms in western Kansas and thus had a place to live and food to eat. Our family helped, too, as they could. My mother, fearing that we didn't have enough to eat, even went so far as to send me a live Rhode Island Red rooster named "Singing Sam." Once he arrived in Lawrence, Sam's song soon ended, and he did make a difference.

Graduation day from law school in Lawrence.

5
Some Early Cases

O nce upon a time I had the illusion that a person accused or convicted of a crime was a separate breed from the rest of us, that he or she probably had two horns and a tail, and was something different and apart. I soon disabused myself of that kind of notion when I found that many criminal defendants were actually just weak individuals, looked just like a million other persons, and had no particular characteristics different from anyone else. Instead, they had, through some force of circumstances or some situation, fallen into trouble and couldn't get out.

Bob and I as we started our careers right out of school, he as bacteriologist and me as a lawyer.

Momma's boy

I was appointed to defend a chap who had written a bunch of bad checks in the Albuquerque area. He had a long FBI rap sheet, indicating that he had 'hung paper,' or written bad checks, in many parts of the U.S. He had no chance of avoiding serving some time because of these checks and his long record. He had no friends or allies in the world except for his 86-year-old mother, who lived in Gary, Indiana. He pled guilty and was sentenced to serve time in the State Penitentiary in Santa Fe.

One afternoon I had a call from the man's elderly mother, who said that ever since he was young her son had spent most of his life in various institutions, all around the country. Her greatest wish was to come to Albuquerque to visit her son before he was sent away to Santa Fe. She said she knew she would have to visit with him in jail but if there were any way he could remain in Albuquerque until she could fly out from Indiana she would be eternally grateful.

I went downtown and talked with District Judge John B. McManus, requesting that the man be kept in the Bernalillo County Jail until his mother could come to visit him. Judge McManus advised me, and properly so, that my client was really in the custody of the County Sheriff and to go take up the matter with him. Whatever the Sheriff decided would be fine with him.

But, as so often happens, there was a twist to the tale. When I met with the Sheriff, he shook his head and said, "Well, Counselor, I would certainly like to oblige you, but this man is sodomizing everybody in my jail. I've got to get him out of here!"

We settled this matter after my client agreed to spend a couple of days in solitary confinement until his mother arrived for her visit.

This kind of situation and others that followed eventually stripped away many of my fantasies about the practice of law, and if a fight went from the abstract heights down into the gutter, I learned as a survivor that I might have to go down and combat it on that basis. Despite this, I never found it necessary to destroy an adversary in a lawsuit, regardless of all my colleagues' frequent comments about me being tough in court. Only once did I purposely pulverize my opponent, and did it rather well, but it wasn't worth the toll it took. I soon learned that there is always more than a single way to present evidence, that the lawsuit is important, but also that you can win it without destroying either your brother attorney or your client's opponent. You can successfully introduce evidence in a manner that does not necessitate taking people apart personally.

Through the years I finally have lost a good bit of the "greenness" that I brought to the practice of law. My mother liked to tease me about being "green as a gourd." The only way to learn how to practice law is to do it, and I have. I've had marvelous help and mentors along the line who permitted me to survive the practice of law to this day. It is indeed a learned profession and as time has gone by I have learned to still venerate the position of the bench and members of the Bar.

My standard and credo of never turning down anybody who had a case and needed legal help was modified from time to time because I would never accept the defense of, nor represent, anyone who was charged with crimes against a child or charged with crimes of violence against a person. However, I often received cases of people who needed help or whose cases had been mishandled and their property lost or their goods taken from them before they happened to end up in my office. I never turned such people down; instead I outlined to them the possibilities—sometimes the possibilities seemed nil—but I never admitted that I couldn't do anything. So, if it actually seemed impossible to help them, it would just take a little longer.

The Good Reverend

My feelings about protecting children may well have gone back to an early incident when I was a child in Eureka. A neighbor literally dragged me home by the scruff of my neck and told my mother that I had been harassing the local minister. I was about eight at the time. She told my mother, "Minta Mary was roller-skating in front, then behind and all around, the Reverend, and would not stop, all up and down Main Street. She was haranguing and harassing that poor man—isn't terrible!"

My mother turned white and shook me—"What on earth made you

do that?" she asked. Clearly I had ruined my family's reputation and was on a one-way fast train bound for Hell. After I caught my breath, I explained that the Reverend had offered me a quarter to kiss him, and I had refused. I had also learned that he had asked many other little girls for a kiss, and also offered each of them a quarter. This just didn't seem right, so I guess I took it to the streets. My mother was mortified to learn about our well-respected minister's darker side, and pretty quickly, as the word spread, he left town, never to be heard of again.

I was about eight when I had my run-in with The Good Reverend.

When to throw a fit

Although I wince when admitting it, when nothing else worked, I accomplished many good results by throwing a tantrum—in the right setting. Deep down I deplore such tactics because in a way it is a prostitution of being a female to use devices like hysterics. However, in some situations it was the only thing that would work. One case really demonstrated this.

A woman who had been traveling on the bus for four days with her very sick infant came into the office. She had traveled to New Mexico to be with her husband and her brother, both of whom were in jail in Albuquerque.

The two men had stolen a car in New Orleans, driven across the state line, and in due course were arrested and charged with interstate transportation of a stolen motor vehicle.

By the time the poor woman arrived in Albuquerque on the bus with her child, her husband and brother had already waived extradition and had been sent back to New Orleans. The woman told me that in order to get to Albuquerque, she had farmed out her other children to neighbors to watch, and had sold all her furniture to pay for the bus fare. By the time she reached my office she was completely out of money and hadn't had anything to eat for days. The sheriff sent her to me because he didn't know what else to do with the poor woman. So, I went down to the sheriff's office and asked him to transport the lady and her baby over to Bernalillo County Medical Center (BCMC) because by now the baby had a very high fever, a troubling deep cough, and obviously had pneumonia. BCMC, the county hospital, often took in people who were unable to pay for medical care. The sheriff told me he'd "be damned if he would take that brat to the hospital because suppose the kid died on the way to the hospital" and someone sued him?

And it was about that time that the roof went off the office, and I yelled, "Well, by God, you get me an ambulance!" Right away the sheriff called for an ambulance, and the mother and the baby were sent on up to BCMC. We called a nun at St. Anthony's Boys' Home, and the home provided housing, room, and some board for the mother until her child could be released from the hospital. We then implored Miss Luther, who ran the Travelers' Aid Society, for transportation money and a little trip money, and the mother and baby got back home safely to New Orleans.

I came to several points like this.

Quit-claim deeds

My good friend, the late John Simms Sr., created a real estate contract that is still being used in New Mexico. It provided a three-way arrangement whereby the property seller would prepare a deed to the property to be sold to be placed in escrow. The buyer would prepare and execute a quit-claim deed back to the seller, and the real estate contract generally provided for the down payment and monthly payments. It had a clause generally providing for 30-day default, which meant that if a payment under the land contract was due and owing for a 30-day period, no matter what equity the buyer might have in the property, the seller could make an affidavit that payment hadn't been made. He could claim that he had served the buyer with a written notice of default demanding that either the payments that were due or, as an alternative, he could demand that the entire amount was due. If the people did not make the payment, upon the affidavit to the bank or the escrow agents all the paperwork was handed back to the seller.

The seller then recorded a quit-claim deed that had been given in advance by the buyer and the buyer was subject to immediate eviction under the law because his rights had been terminated. Now, as odd as it may seem, people who were the buyers and who fell into default (for any reason) and received a written notice that they were in default were given 30 days to cure the default. If they didn't pay the amount, they would be evicted and their rights would be terminated. Often they actually just moved off the property because they had received a notice telling them to do so. Early on, this happened a great deal. That's when you needed to throw the people out. I'm happy to say that the conscience of the courts has prevented this kind of hardship in many instances where court action has had to be brought to cause the eviction of the buyers who fell into default, for whatever reason.

I've always felt that the poor and people who were not able to take care of themselves need a friend in a higher place. I've never been in a high place but I have tried to have access to some high places in order to help some of these people even up the odds. I believe you ought to pick on someone your own size and not destroy people—instead, you owe some duty or at least some degree of fairness to everyone.

Dealing with a dealer

One grievous and memorable case involved a young man who went to a used car lot and bought a convertible coupe. He made a down payment and signed a note for the balance. The salesman put a new top on the convertible, and made a second, new note, payable at exorbitant interest, for the top. Then the contract provided that although the vehicle was sold "as is," should any repairs be made, that 50% of the repairs would be paid for by the dealer during the first 30 days or 500 miles the car was driven. My client had driven the car less than half a block off the used car lot when it stopped dead and had to be towed back to the dealership's shop. My young client was told that the total repair would cost $120, and that $60 of that was his bill. So he signed a third note for the $60 repair bill. The truth of the matter was that there was a $15 part in the ignition system that had been added, and the car went on its merry way.

Well, it seemed to me that this was a classic place to take on this particular automobile dealer, which we did. It was clearly fraud upon this unknowing kid who was just working for a living. I was able, by dint of threatening almost anything under the sun, and anything else I could think of, to get this deal set aside and to help the young man to return the car to the dealer, clean up these atrocious contracts, and let the young man find a reasonable automobile from a reputable dealer. And it worked.

Not all of these rather shaky adventures had a successful result. For example, one client, a young man, was living in his automobile. It was the only home he had and he stored all his gear—his clothing, a few small household utensils and what little he had—in the trunk. The car was financed by Beneficial Finance Company. The young man fell behind in his payments. One day he came back to where the car was usually parked and found it had been towed away by the finance company. Proceedings were already underway to sell the car at wholesale and to get a default judgment against the young man. All of his personal effects had been thrown into a couple of big cardboard cartons. The only reason we were able to get these personal effects back was because they had no value to the finance company, which was only interested in recouping what it could get out of the defaulted loan.

However, something was missing from the cartons. The young man told me he had lost the family Bible, and that he had three $100 bills hidden in the Bible, and this was his stash. When I asked him where he got the $300 he said he had won it in a crap game, and I believed him. The upshot was that we could never convince the finance company that there had ever been any money in the Bible, for whoever picked up the car had done a pretty good job of scrounging through the young man's things. I truly believed the money had been in that family Bible.

WWJD

Another memorable battle was with the Archbishop of Santa Fe. We were attempting to change the Catholic Church's general ruling that suicide victims could not be buried in the Church cemetery. A client's son, who had been found dead in Juarez, Mexico, from an apparent drug overdose, could not be buried in "hallowed ground" because of the suspicion that he may have taken his own life. My client, who had worked all of her adult life in a local laundry, ironing literally thousands of garments, and over all those years had faithfully tithed to the Church, as much as her means would allow. She sadly said that it looked to her like it was no use being Catholic; you might just as well be a Baptist.

A Star Chamber affair

Another case was maddening and terrifying at the same time, and was a modern-day Star Chamber affair. (The Star Chamber was an English court of law where court sessions were held in secret, with no indictments, no right of appeal, no juries, and no witnesses. Over time it became a symbol of the misuse and abuse by the English monarchy and courts.)

My client had been a cartographer with the Department of Agriculture for many years and was near retirement when she was served with a notice of termination because of her "Association with known communists." We requested a hearing, and got one. The hearing was conducted in the old U.S. Courthouse. It was entirely secret—the press was barred from covering the hearing, and the windows of both doors into the courtroom and other windows of the courthouse were papered over.

The man who conducted this hearing was a cloak and dagger type, and even wore a slouch hat and a trench coat, just like you'd see a foreign agent wear in the movies. A close girlfriend of my client had turned her in to the Department of Agriculture for "consorting with known communists."

The girlfriend, along with my client, had actually shared the amours of a high-ranking New Mexico politician. Upon their falling-out as friends, the girlfriend turned my client in to the government as being "friendly to communists." While today this would be seen as outrageous, this occurred during the McCarthy era and actually about the same time that U.S. Senator Joseph McCarthy held his televised investigation into communist influences in the Army.

Our hearing went on for three days, during which the complete dossier on my client was revealed—it was about the size of two Sears and Roebuck catalogs. I was not allowed to cross-examine. No witnesses appeared against her, and I will never forget one of the questions asked by the interrogator: "Do you recall a meeting in Los Alamos, New Mexico, during which you gave a dollar to the Henry A. Wallace campaign?" Since there was no way to cross-examine witnesses, my client had no way to confront the person or persons who turned her in for being a "known communist sympathizer." My client had never gone to college and had an inordinate admiration for anybody with a higher education than her own. As a result she had fallen under the spell of a group of Los Alamos intelligentsia, among whom may have been people sympathetic to the Wallace campaign.

When the three-day hearing ended, I was exhausted, frightened of the consequences of this kind of an inquisition, and in closing said to the main Inquisitor, "Sir, I have the dubious pleasure of telling you that you are without doubt the meanest son of a bitch I have ever had any contact with in my life. That is all."

During the time this hearing was going on I began to receive masses of communist literature at my home. At the same time a trial of a communist sympathizer was being conducted in the Federal Court in Denver. For a long time afterward, I continued to receive all of this communist literature until I asked the Post Office to stop sending any of this stuff to my office or to my home.

One of the most frightening events that occurred while I was representing my client was coming home to our farm to find the gate posts at the end of our long driveway painted bright red. This really was the topper. I was terrified that I was being targeted, and now my family was being targeted as well.

Not long afterward, a good friend who lived in town helped break the spell and get us back to normal. She mentioned that it was always hard to find our farm in Corrales, so she and a friend had painted our gate posts bright red—now they could always find us.

6

CORRALES

The sudden appearance of the mysterious red gate posts at the end of our driveway was just another day in the life on our Corrales farm. After a short time on Guadalupe Trail, we moved over the Rio Grande River into the heart of Corrales. Early in the 1950s, we bought a house and 27 acres, a long, narrow strip of land that ran from Corrales Road, then gravel and dirt, all the way to the sand hills of the west mesa.

Our home in Corrales.

Today it is a little hard to imagine that not so long ago the sand hills that are covered by Rio Rancho homes and businesses once were empty, all the way from Central Avenue on the south to Bernalillo on the north. Corrales is now a bedroom community of Albuquerque, and electronic giant Intel's parking lot rests at the west end of our old property. In those days, Corrales was made up of small farms that made a long strip of green all along the west side of the Rio Grande. Our neighbors grew chili, apples, and alfalfa, and everyone had their own vegetable gardens. The area called Corrales actually was very historic, and its name purportedly came from the corrals along the river where Spanish soldiers once kept their horses.

We bought a small adobe house, then unplastered inside and out. It was made of *terrones,* which are adobe bricks with straw added, which improves the insulation. Our single-story three-room house had a few small windows, one bathroom, and a floor of crooked wooden planks. The first thing we noticed was that the straw and mud walls were home to all sorts of creatures, including centipedes. You had to take care to shake out your shoes and jeans before putting them on. At least we didn't have one of our neighbor's problem: centipedes nested in her ceiling and had a nasty habit of dropping down onto her bed in the middle of the night.

The farm had three ancient apple orchards and a few other fruit trees, and a giant cottonwood tree in the front yard. The tree was well over a hundred years old and the house dated back more than two hundred years. While we lived in a very historic area, we hadn't chosen the farm because of this. We chose the land because it was a good buy, and it gave my husband a chance to fulfill his dream of having a small farm. This definitely was not a gentleman's farm but a working farm. The little farm also had alfalfa fields, and wild asparagus sprouts leapt up in one orchard each summer. Wild grapes grew on the ditch bank.

In those early days, before we drilled our irrigation well, all the water for the orchards and fields came from a drainage ditch that divided our land into two nearly equal parts. The irrigation system was part of the ancient *acequia,* or irrigation ditch, a system of ditches dating back to the 16th century. The ditch ran high and full after the rain fell up north, and the water was often Jemez-red, reflecting the red soil around Jemez Pueblo. The property was long and narrow, just like many farms that had been part of the original Spanish land grants. It was a longtime custom with these old land grants for families to divide the land equally among the children, and as time went along, the strips of rich farmland grew narrower and narrower—we jokingly called them "the spaghetti farms."

We had many wonderful neighbors. To the south were Betty McKee, the Gilchrist family, the photographer Rosie Rosenthal, and the Woolletts. To the north were the Nutters, with their school bus company, then Gene and Mary Merriam. The Merriams were among the first to use new ways to grow vegetables and in effect were the first organic farmers we knew. The Arundales, a little further north, raised pigs just like we did, and were involved in many community activities, including the 4-H Club. Mabel Arundale later was the official Avon lady for Corrales, and drove up and down the muddy driveways in her little Scout. The Arundales' house was like a second home to our kids, who played with Tom and Pat every day. The Woolletts, who had a family of five children, several of whom were our kids' playmates, lived in a historic hacienda built around a center courtyard and swimming pool. On Halloween the Woolletts turned their barn into a haunted house, to the delight of all the neighbors. A little further north up Corrales Road was the Weaver family, who had a white and green Victorian style home among all the adobes. To the east, across Corrales Road were our friends the Rutherfords and Mr. Crist, a children's photographer.

Three of the Dunlap kids in Corrales. Left: Robert A. Dunlap, Jr.; center: Mary Katherine Dunlap, 9; and right: Elizabeth Jean Dunlap, 3.

Our oldest son, Sheldon Lee, joined the Air Force when he was 19.

In time we had a nearly self-sufficient farm, with chickens, pigs, rabbits, turkeys, ducks, cows, calves, and a few horses. Oh, and occasionally we had a visit from our neighbors' strutting peacocks. In one corner of the living room was an old bookcase originally owned by Elfego Baca. We also had telephone service and were members of a huge party line, but almost no one called us before dropping by. Friends and strangers alike assumed they were welcome and that they would find us at home. The doors were never locked in those days, so you never knew who might be waiting for you when you came home. And, although we were far out of Albuquerque, we had a steady stream of visitors, particularly on Sundays around lunch time.

Our chickens were only a small part of a real menagerie.

Nearly everyone in Corrales and in the North Valley grew their own fruits and vegetables and part of that also involved canning and freezing your own food. The little kitchen was filled with canning jars and bubbling hot water, and my husband experimented with making jerky and cheese and apple cider. The cheddar cheese rounds and venison jerky found places in the bedroom—the jerky hung on a long string near the ceiling and the often-green cheddar wheel graced a bookshelf. Our few dairy cows produced very rich milk and cream, and we made cottage cheese in the old way—boiled first on the stove, then hung on the clothesline in cheesecloth bags or at times a pillowcase would do just fine. Bob ground oats to make oatmeal. We also butchered hogs and steers, and any neighbors who helped always took home part of the meat—that was and probably still is the tradition. The chickens laid eggs that my son Bob sold in a very successful egg route, and chickens also made delicious fried chicken on Sundays. We also baled alfalfa when we had enough of a crop.

So, in addition to our full-time careers, Bob and I became small farmers. Even as our little family grew to six with Elizabeth Jean, this meant early farm hours, long work hours in Albuquerque, and, at the end of the workday, a return to long farm hours.

People always seemed to find us in Corrales—one was the Watkins man. He was the most persistent peddler we had ever seen. He walked all the way up our dusty drive calling out as loudly as he could, "HELLOOOO-EW MRS. DUNLAP..." or when he had no answer, "HELL-EW THE HOUSE...?" Although the kids would hide, he looked all around and sure enough would find us—so our pantry was always well stocked with Watkins vanilla, cinnamon, and the other spices he sold.

My office was about 20 miles away in north Albuquerque, over Corrales Road, which was then a bumpy gravel road, which ran over an old trestle bridge with its wooden planks spanning the Rio Grande River. If you drove up to our house, you might be greeted by a small flock of Muscovy ducks or a cranky tom turkey, two or more friendly dogs, and an occasional runaway horse. You might also come on a day when the two hundred or so pigs decided to break out of their pens and run to the north. A few wild things wandered by, too. We never could stop the regular migration of skunks down a "skunk trail" that is still there today and is still well used, from what we have heard. We never knew exactly when our striped friends started this trail. My husband rigged up a rope snare that would throw them high in the air; and he then would shoot them and give the hides to our Indian friends, who used the skins in ceremonies.

We started with a herd of ordinary Hereford cattle but eventually my husband was able to build up a beautiful herd of 99.9% purebred Charolais cattle. His first bull was nicknamed "Louie"; I won't bother to give the rest of his official name, but I would say that his lineage was much more royal than any of ours. Though he was huge, weighing about two tons, Louie was very gentle and became almost a pet. My older daughter would climb up and ride him around the corral. He never knew a fence he couldn't push over and wandered more or less at will up and down the irrigation ditch—to the great delight of some of the family cows, and unquestionably improved the breed.

We had some outside help with larger projects such as irrigating the orchards and alfalfa fields. Our helpers were usually from Jemez Pueblo or Zia Pueblo, and were very adept at directing the water from the main irrigation ditch down to the respective fields. One of our favorites was Johnny Yepa, from Jemez. Johnny was very funny and a real prankster. When my sisters and mother came to visit from Kansas, Johnny told the "palominas," as he called them because of their fair skin and blonde hair, that "wild Indians" were still around, and that the Indians kept their tomahawks in the cottonwood tree in front of our house. Johnny braided his hair in a long pigtail that he called his "chongo," which is Spanish for "monkey."

Our first and last cocktail party in Corrales

Johnny and his wife Maria would also drop in for a visit whenever they were in the area and, as was their custom, felt fine about just coming in the house and making themselves comfortable. We had no locks on the doors and they had none on their doors at Jemez, either.

The Yepas also played an unwitting part in the one and only "cocktail party" we had for some of my fellow Albuquerque lawyers. My husband and I planned a barbecue in our front yard, under the old cottonwood, and went to great pains to build a barbeque pit out of blocks, to get tables and chairs, and the best beef possible. Anyway, the lawyers all found us, and the party was going strong—my first social event, and the laughter and music were everywhere.

Then, out of the corner of my eye, I saw the Yepas wandering up our drive—unfortunately, both had stopped by the local bar for a couple of bottles of wine and had had drunk most of it by the time they staggered up the drive. Before we knew it, they were headed for the front door, and were now arguing loudly, shoving each other, and then they both collapsed, and fell into a deep sleep head to head in the doorway. Our guests didn't miss a beat—they merely carefully stepped over Johnny and Maria the rest of the evening. No one ever said a word about my visitors, but it was the first and last big social legal party we ever had.

Grandma has a guest

We also had many other friends from the pueblos, including one of our favorite couples, Tony and Lucy from Zia Pueblo. Tony was a gentle giant with a wicked sense of humor, dark-skinned and dark-eyed. Lucy was tiny, about 4'11" at most, with delicate features, but all we knew who ruled the roost.

My family members from Kansas always had adventures when they came to visit, and none more than my mother, who told everyone that we lived in Mexico, not New Mexico. One day on her first visit to Corrales, and while all we Dunlaps were at work and school, our friend Tony dropped by for a visit. My mother was in the kitchen, and happened to look out the little front window. She was terrified to see a tall, very dark-skinned Indian man striding toward the front door. Grandma herself was nearly six feet tall and a very strong 200 pounds, but Tony easily towered over her. Tony knocked, and Grandma peered around the door. Tony could see that she was frightened, and he just couldn't help himself. He put on the fiercest warrior face he had and grunted at her—probably the equivalent of "Ugh" like in the Western movies—and stepped inside.

My mother was terrified, but what could she do? What she did was turn to food—we always used food for every crisis, and she immediately began bringing out anything that was edible in the house. She was no shrinking violet and not afraid of much on earth, but this was different. Tony was the first real American Indian she had seen. And, he was so tall and dark and fierce—well, all she could think of was how to try to survive.

Tony grunted in his great big voice and Grandma brought out another dish, and another and another. Tony pretended that he didn't like the taste of any of them, so she brought out something else—maybe canned peaches would work. Tony said something that sounded like Ugh, so she tried something else—apple pie? Ugh. Ham slices? Ugh. She brought out a glass of iced tea. Snort, Ugh. He pounded the table. Finally Faye played her last trump card—she brought out her renowned angel food cake, which was just cooling. The recipe, which called for 18 eggs, was a well-kept secret until the very end of her life.

Tony later told us he could barely keep from falling off the chair with laughter as all the dishes were paraded out. He gave Faye a fierce look, and grabbed a piece of the cake. "UMMM"—then he grabbed the entire cake, pan and all, and stomped out the door to his truck and drove away. Faye had survived.

I didn't know whether to laugh or cry when we got home and heard her tale of woe. I don't think she ever got over it, even though Tony did come by to apologize. To Faye's astonishment, Tony apologized in beautiful English. I think she forgave him, but was never sure.

My husband's dream of a small farm gradually grew into herds of pigs, hutches of rabbits, flocks of ducks, gaggles of geese, flocks of chickens, more and more cows, and always a few horses. Robert had a formula for choosing livestock: four sheep ate just as much as two cows and a single horse; thus, a horse was pretty much worthless. As with any farm, everyone pitched in. And, true to form, we also had a few animal disasters, such as a fire in the hog houses that killed 64 pigs, large and small. We buried them in the sand hills at the end of our property at the end of what is Intel's parking lot on the west mesa. A rabbit plague emptied most of the hutches, and a German shepherd killed most of the chickens, even those the skunks managed to miss.

Each time we had one of these disasters, we blinked and started up again—at one time we had more than 200 pigs and it was a challenge to keep them fed. We bought day-old bread from the Rainbow Bakery and cream and milk from Creamland Dairies, mixing the two and feeding the hogs twice a day. Before we had a truck, we used the Pontiac coupe to bring the bread home, packing the back seat and trunk area full of loaves and pastries. The kids feasted on the pastries on the ride home from Albuquerque. The horses and cows grazed on our alfalfa, and the rabbits and chickens got feed from the feed store. The days were long because we fed all the animals, then ourselves, got the kids off to school, and Robert and I were off to work in Albuquerque. The farm life was the other half of my life—I wore two hats for a long time, as a farm wife and as a lawyer. It wasn't unusual for me to load up a truck full of pigs and drive them to market before going on to court. The days were long but I also loved the beauty of the Rio Grande Valley and the many adventures we had there.

The widow of Corrales

I tried very hard to keep a distance between my law practice and clients and my family, but even so, more than one client would seek me out at home. Dinnertime was a good time to catch us, of course. One of my clients was a widow with seven children, who did ironing for a living and usually managed to consume at least a half-gallon bottle of Gilby's gin every day. She lived up in the sand hills, not too far from us, and had an unfortunate habit of catching us right at dinner. One evening, as we were just starting our dinner, a small child raced in the front door, grabbed a watermelon off our kitchen shelf, and raced back out to the widow's car without saying a word.

I shared her problems with an assistant pastor of the Church of the Nativity of the Blessed Virgin in Alameda. He took care of her spiritual problems and I took care, as best I could, of her various legal problems, of which there were many.

Her last child, the seventh, was born nine months after her latest lover had been rebuffed when she changed all the locks on the house and barred the doors and windows against him. The fellow procured a ladder, climbed up to the second-story window, and climbed in the window like the Don Juan he apparently was. The last little child arrived some nine months later.

One day at noon, the pastor called me from his home, and told me that my client was driving her old station wagon down the street, far beyond the speed limit, weaving from side to side across the road. He knew that she was drunk, and felt it was my particular province to run her down and get her off the highway. He remarked that he would have helped but that this situation was not a "spiritual thing," it was part of my jurisdiction as her lawyer. And, he explained, anyway, he had an appointment to go to try to convert Mrs. B, a wealthy widow, to the Catholic faith and didn't have time to take care of the widow of Corrales.

7

A NEW OFFICE ADDRESS

I moved my law office downtown, to the old Rosenwald Building at the corner of Fourth Street and Central Avenue.

The Rosenwald Building.
Some of the tenants
had wings.

The building housed a dime store downstairs and had a few govern-ment offices on the second floor. The entry to the building led to an area with a high vaulted ceiling. Whoever was the first person in the building in the morning had the task of shooing the bats out. The bats made their home up along the ceiling in the old building.

I rented a closet-sized office on the third floor, in Suite 303, which was already occupied by Judge Irwin S. Moise, a former District Judge and future chief justice of the New Mexico Supreme Court and attorneys Louis R. (Lew) Sutin and Jack Leftow. I was neither a member of their firm nor associated with them, except in a geographical sense, but we all had a fine time and many adventures over the years. Judge Moise became kind of an involuntary mentor to me, and many times I imposed upon his fine judg-ment and advice.

One time I told Judge Moise that one of my opponents reminded me of a windmill because he flailed around so much, and I felt he was an extremely incompetent lawyer. Judge Moise just laughed and added, "Never underestimate your opponent—even a blind sow may sometimes root up an acorn."

Alienation of affections

I had a referral from the Bar Association Referral Service of a case involving alienation of affections. "Alienation of Affections" is a respectable court action based in English Common Law. One could claim damages against a defendant for enticing away a wife, a servant, or other people under the protection of the plaintiff. Although the plaintiff is usually a spouse, others can also be charged, including clergymen and family members.

The facts of this case proved to be quite salacious: While the plaintiff's wife was at work, she and the store manager were often seen making love in the company freight elevator as it moved up and down between the floors. Some of the couple's activities were, at least for those times, deemed to be inappropriate and sometimes downright perverse.

I didn't want to touch this case with a 10-foot pole, and asked Judge Moise how he would recommend getting rid of it. He replied, "It's really very easy. It's kind of a crank case, and the thing to do is to write to this prospective plaintiff and demand a retainer of $250. That will shut him up, and you'll never hear from him again."

So, acting as usual upon Judge Moise's good advice, I did write a letter to the prospective plaintiff, telling him that because of the nature of the case and the necessity for additional investigation, I would require an advance retainer of $500. I thought, if $250 might stop him, $500 certainly will. Perish the thought! I immediately got back a certified check for $500.

When I came into the office on Monday morning, a very irate Lebanese man was waiting for me. He said, "I came down here to see what my lawyer looked like, and to see if I liked her or not." I said, "Well, what do you think?" I was hoping he didn't like women lawyers and I could just hand back his check and get out of this one. Unfortunately, he said, "Well I like your looks and I want to go ahead with the case." So the fat was in the fire.

Well, the story did have a happy ending. About the time I filed the lawsuit I was appointed Judge of the Small Claims Court. I was able to hand this case on to a colleague, who handled it with relish—and with some financial reward for our disgruntled client.

A scientist on Saturday

Early one Saturday morning, as I was working away in Suite 303, one of the most eminent, world-class physicists from Los Alamos wandered in off the street. He needed some property matters handled, he said.

When I asked who had referred him to me, he said he had seen my sign in the window and just walked in. I warned this delightful and charming man about the dangers of just walking in off the street to work with an unknown lawyer—he might have gotten a poor lawyer, instead of me. At least I could do a competent job of handling his property matters. He laughed heartily and told me that any lawyer honest enough to be working early on a Saturday morning was good enough for him.

The scientist had designed and directed the building of the medical laboratory at Los Alamos. He told me in great detail about the devotion he and his team had to the job and the experiments they were performing. He didn't tell me anything about the actual experiments, of course, but indicated that once he and his team began an experiment or project, it became the only thing in their lives. They literally lived in the laboratory; they never shaved or bathed very often; they didn't go home on any regular schedule; and he said the team never left the laboratory for weeks at a time. They ate only if they remembered to, and were completely devoted to and absorbed in their important work.

The physicist realized that this was no life for his wife and family, and asked me to arrange a fair property settlement for them.

Although my association with this man was casual, and limited to this one occasion, I felt a real sense of loss when I learned that he was killed in an airplane crash while en route with his associates to Brussels for a nuclear symposium. This charming man did not seem to fit in with our ordinary world, where he certainly would not have walked in to get a complex property matter handled by whomever he happened to find working on a Saturday morning.

A bad contract

Answering a call to go down to meet an elderly client, I got up my courage and went down to the White House Rooms. The White House Rooms Hotel was located on the second floor of a dilapidated old building, right across from Santa Fe Train Depot. In the kindest of terms, the White House Rooms was a flophouse. It was flanked on one side by Doc's Bar and on the other side by a restaurant that kept its chickens hanging in the window for three or four days at a time.

I walked around the block about three times before I had the courage to walk in. When I opened the front door, two winos literally rolled out into the street. I gritted my teeth, stepped over the men—who might as well have been dead for all I could tell, and went upstairs.

The White House Rooms still had chamber pots under the beds, and it was said that the beds were always warm, with or without blankets; most of them were occupied around the clock, and rented by the hour.

This case involved one of the worst kinds of contracts I encountered in New Mexico. This was a contract made by an aged parent with one of his children. In exchange for taking care of the parent for the rest of his or her life, the child would be given the deed to the elderly parent's property.

My client was a tiny elderly woman whose grandson had forced her to deed her property, located out in the country, over to him. He did advance her a small amount of money—for which he should have had a mortgage, perhaps, but never the deed to her property. This seemed to be a common thing, particularly among the various Hispanic clients that I encountered. I found these contracts to be vicious, and in many cases they immediately caused great dissension in the family because the aged parent was not always properly cared for. Instead, the parent was often neglected and even abandoned after the deed was signed over. As I talked with the tiny lady, I learned that she literally had no place to stay, and had been taken in by the kindly folks who ran the White House Rooms. She served as a kind of chambermaid there, and was allowed to cook her meals in the proprietors' small kitchenette.

Her grandson was a youth counselor and one of the most prominent citizens of Corrales. After we filed suit against the grandson, we were able to set aside the deed, and reinstate this little woman back to her property and home. Still, I will never forget the sight of her grandson, the outstanding citizen, sitting on the witness stand. He told me proudly, "I figured someone was going to get something out of the old lady's property, and it might as well be me."

Jose X

I had good reason to set another of these contracts aside, even after one of my brothers at law had made it. It concerned a wonderful old Hispanic gentleman, Jose X. Lucero, who died of pneumonia at the age of 97 after spending a cold November night on a bench in the Plaza at Old Town. He had had a fight with his daughter-in-law and refused to come home to bed. Instead, he spent that cold and final winter night on the park bench.

Mr. Lucero had been an early-day jailer in New Mexico. He described how in 1912, for example, prisoners often were tied standing up. They were tied to a tall wagon wheel, where they were left for 24 or even more hours until they could be transported somewhere to a jail. He also said that in those days the prisoners were furnished women in their cells. He told me "This helped them have a better attitude." (Interestingly enough, in the Bernalillo County jail in the early 1950s certain prostitutes openly worked the jail, without being prosecuted.) Mr. Lucero had also freighted goods with oxen and a wagon across the Rio Grande River when it was deep enough in winter to have six feet of solid ice. He had two families, his regular family and a closet *chiquita,* with a complete second family, including several children. He openly acknowledged all the members of this second family, all of whom were listed in the Church records.

Mr. Lucero's troubles began after he had become angry at his daughter and had gone to live with his son and daughter-in-law. The contract that had been made by their family attorney provided that the old gentleman would be cared for all the rest of his life by his daughter-in-law and his son. I should add that Jose X was a very difficult old gentleman. He was cantankerous, and, as I knew only too well, hard to handle. For example, on one occasion when the New Mexico Historical Society sent down a person to interview Mr. Lucero, he promptly bodily picked up the interviewer and threw him out the door. The would-be historian's tape recorder soon sailed out after the erstwhile interviewer.

Despite his difficult personality, I found I really liked the old man. He was a beautiful gnarled old fellow who reminded me of my own grandfather, with one exception—his skin was a handsome coffee-color instead of the white skin of my very German Grandfather Kramm. Mr. Lucero was the child of a Spanish mother and an immigrant German peddler who had come through the country with all his worldly goods in a sack on his back. I once asked Mr. Lucero if his middle name was "Xavier," and he bent over laughing. He told me that no, he had never learned to read or write, and that he had transferred lots of property in the state and he always did it with an X and whoever drew the deed put in the Jose and Lucero and the X was always in the middle. When Mr. Lucero finally learned to write his name, he felt the X "looked so pretty in the middle" that he left it in. He had no middle name at all.

The old man liked to tease and always promised to take me to a dance. Even as his health was failing, he was jolly enough to say that he and I "should take in a dance one of these days."

The Nazareth Hospital beat

Thanks to all the referrals I received from Judge Simms' office, I had almost a regular beat at Nazareth Hospital and Sanitarium, north of Albuquerque. The hospital was run by the Catholic sisters and it offered treatment not only of mental illness but had an alcohol treatment program as well. Of course, many of the patients were tuberculosis patients who came to the Southwest for the climate.

One of the most intriguing clients I met at Nazareth Hospital was a doctor, a German-Jewish refugee who had escaped Nazi Germany with his

Steinway grand piano, an umbrella, and a pistol. He was a celebrated chest surgeon and had made his way to Albuquerque after the war. He was hired to operate the traveling x-ray units that traveled throughout the state. He was not licensed or certified to practice as a chest physician in the U.S. The doctor had until recently lived at Fort Stanton Hospital, the headquarters of the x-ray unit program.

One morning the doctor came down to breakfast brandishing his pistol. While he waved the pistol around he told all the members of the staff who were in the dining hall that he was tired of being mistreated and discriminated against by them and that he was going to "take some of them out" with his pistol. Luckily he was subdued and instead of going through the regular procedure of being sent to the state mental hospital in Las Vegas, because he was a physician he was given free treatment in Nazareth Sanitarium. Just before his breakdown, he had bought a new Oldsmobile, and the car was sitting in the garage at the Sanitarium moldering away on its tires.

As a professional courtesy, the doctor was given all his medical treatment free—including a series of electroshock treatments—but was expected to pay his own board bill. He of course had no way to do this and no funds, so in speaking with his guardian, we suggested that the Oldsmobile might be appraised and sold for the highest price possible, and the money held for the doctor. He could then use it to pay his board bill, at least as far as it could go.

Of course, this was not as easy as it sounded, because Sister, the hospital administrator, would not permit the car to be taken off the hospital grounds for the appraisal. And, I couldn't get any automobile dealer to come out to take a look at the automobile to make the appraisal. Finally, we got over the stalemate. The doctor's car was sold privately at a reasonable price and the money was applied to his board bill.

One day when I visited him, I found that he was in much worse shape than at my last visit. He confided in me that after one of his shock treatments, he had awakened to find that a crucifix had been placed around his neck. This had such an immediate and powerfully traumatic effect on him that it caused a relapse. He finally recovered enough to be discharged from the hospital and went on with his affairs. Before he left, he gave me a forwarding address, and asked me to mail his umbrella to him. I discovered that trying to mail an umbrella with the post office regulations of the time was even more difficult than advising him and taking care of his guardianship matters! Although we never learned what happened to him, we could only wish that the last part of his life brought him some peace.

Ruby, ruby

Another Nazareth client was the wife of one of the chief engineers of the Colorado River Project. She was a lady with a serious alcohol problem. She had been in the Alvarado Hotel one night and had fallen asleep with a lighted cigarette. She set the mattress and her room on fire. After the confusion of the fire and rescue, she had been placed in Nazareth Sanitarium because she was not indigent, and they needed time for her husband to figure out what he wanted to do with her.

When I first met her, she had been in Nazareth Sanitarium for more than a year, and had suddenly decided that she wanted to be released. She called the Simms office, and they asked me to go talk with her. We tried to trace what had happened to her belongings and personal effects, most of which had been scattered after the fire in her hotel room. She was looking for one item in particular, a large diamond and ruby dinner ring that had vanished during the fire. It was very recognizable and she could definitely identify and reclaim it if we had been able to find it. We never found the ring. However, coincidentally, I happened to see a ring that was almost identical to the description of her expensive ring on the finger of one of the detectives employed in the office of the District Attorney.

Family matters

Through the years, I have handled many family matters, some most grievous, and some that were pretty simple and clear-cut. I have always been disturbed by the failure of myself and my fellow lawyers to properly take care of the separate and important interests of the children involved in these matters.

In New Mexico, in the 1950s we never had a system of guardianship for children, unlike states such as New York. There, designated law guardians and trained professionals from appropriate fields looked after the interests of the children.

In New Mexico in those early days, the process we generally used was to ask the court to appoint some young lawyer as guardian for the children in appropriate cases. In some cases, it was particularly difficult to ask the court to refer the matter to the Health and Social Services Division for investigation and for a report to be given to the court by appropriate case workers.

The process of going out in the hall and finding a young attorney to come in and to try to represent the children, when he or she had never talked with them, never seen them, and was not familiar with the file or the family and its background did nothing to foster the interests of the children.

A child has a right to be maintained in almost the same situation financially and socially that he had when he had two parents together, before the family was broken up. I will only touch upon a few of these cases that I became involved in.

A 12-year-old time bomb

I represented a divorcee, a schoolteacher who had custody of her two young sons. Her former husband was an administrator in the Albuquerque public school system. At his request, she had changed her name and her children's so the fact of the divorce wouldn't be an embarrassment to him.

One of her sons, a 12-year-old, attended Lew Wallace School and was a kind of genius for his age, especially in the sciences. Because he was very interested in chemistry, his mother had bought him a complete chemistry set, which he kept at home. And because he was so studious, he was a good target for a group of school bullies. One day, after they had teased and harassed him, he told them if they didn't leave him alone, he would throw sulfuric acid on them. On this particular day, he had gone to his home—which was close to the school—and the bullies followed him, baiting him, calling him a sissy and "four-eyes," and everything else an ultra-smart, introverted, aloof kid is usually called. They followed him up onto his porch. As good as his word, he went inside, got a vial of sulfuric acid, and threw it in the face of the first kid in line.

Luckily, a doctor whose office was in the neighborhood rushed over and rescued the kid who had been burned with the acid. The 12-year-old chemistry whiz was apprehended and handed over to the juvenile authorities.

After psychological and psychiatric testing, he was found to be in need of supervision, and was sent to the State Hospital in Las Vegas. He was placed in a ward with adult male patients because at that time there was no place for children in custody pending a juvenile hearing, particularly a child deemed mentally ill. The father then came forth heroically—although he had never so much as sent the children a postcard after the divorce—and told Judge Edwin L. Swope that he would pay any cost to have his son removed from Las Vegas and sent to the Brown School for Exceptional Children, in San Marcus, Texas.

Soon after the child was sent to Texas, the mother sent a letter to District Judge Edwin L. Swope, which was delivered on Christmas Day. The letter rambled on, "...here you are in the bosom of your family, and you have taken my son away from me, and now I'm alone." The judge found it to be threatening, and called me in as attorney for the mother and the young boy. Furthermore, the District Attorney was called in and, in chambers, the judge said that his life and that of his family might be threatened, and thus asked the District Attorney to declare my client incompetent, and to begin the proceedings to have her committed.

I advised the court that my client was certainly not incompetent, and I was certain that should this sort of *ex parte* procedure be done, that the consequences would be most unfortunate for all involved. I assured the court that my client was not a violent person, and that while she had acted in a manner we couldn't condone, I really did not believe that she was a danger to the court. She was merely a heartbroken mother who missed her son.

Later, my client went to visit with the son, took him out for Sunday dinner, and spirited him back to Ohio, where she had moved. I was neatly called before Judge Swope, who said he found my fine hand in this kidnapping of this child from the Texas school. I assured the judge that I had no part in this, I had no knowledge of it, but I could understand the pressures and worries this mother had. Faced with a contempt of court charge, the matter was finally handled informally in chambers. So far as I know, the son is still living in Ohio with his mother and younger brother.

A mother's choice

My old Lutheran pastor in our small hometown in Kansas, who had taken on a new church in San Diego, sent me a child custody case. A young man, a parishioner of his church, was trying to gain custody of his two-year-old daughter. The child had been carried off to New Mexico by the mother, who reportedly was living with her boyfriend in the mountains near Manzano.

According to what they could learn, the baby girl was being seriously neglected. I accepted the case, and spoke with the young man by telephone, telling him I would let him know when we could get a hearing. I asked him to come to New Mexico for the hearing.

My investigator and I went up to the Manzano Mountains to check things out. We found the two-year-old dressed in rags, playing in a mud puddle outside a cabin. Inside, the mother and her lover were in bed at noon. The small cabin contained a 100-lb sack of dog food for the huge dogs that ranged around the place. They were the only well-fed ones there. Aside from a case of Budweiser, there was no sign of milk or any other food suitable for the child.

Back in Albuquerque, we filed a petition for a writ of habeus corpus, and the matter was set before Judge Robert Reidy. Judge Reidy was particularly hard on any parent who was neglecting, refusing to support, or abusing a child. Although we weren't allowed to pick the particular court for our case, if we had right on our side, we always hoped and prayed that by lot we might be able to get Judge Reidy to handle any case that involved child neglect or abuse.

I called the mother as the first witness and, upon cross-examination, went into the conditions under which they were living up in the mountains. At that point, Judge Reidy interrupted me and turning to the young woman said, "If I asked you to choose between your lover and your child, what would you do? How would you choose?"

Her rejoinder, as she burst into great sobbing tears, was, "I love him, I love him, Judge." The judge stopped the proceedings and said, "I find you to be an unfit mother, and I award custody of the child to the father."

The attorney for the mother rose up in great haste and asked the court to set an appeal bond so he could appeal the matter immediately. Judge Reidy roared that there would be no appeal, and there would be no bond set. He had ruled; he was directing my client to take immediate custody of the little girl, and advised the young father to get in his car and drive right on back to California with the baby. This was the kind of rough and ready justice (if you could call it that) that we got.

A child vanishes

Another child custody matter demonstrated very well how New Mexico justice could operate in those days. Like the young father in the earlier case, my client was also from California. She was the mother of a four-year-old child who was allowed to visit with the paternal grandparents up at La Madera, north of Espanola.

At the end of this particular visit, the mother had arrived to take her daughter home, but the grandparents informed her that the father (from whom she was estranged) had snatched the child and taken her away. They claimed they didn't know where the child was.

We filed a writ of habeus corpus in the District Court at Santa Fe, and I personally took the writ and other papers up to Espanola and handed them to Sheriff Emilio Naranjo, so there would be no question of the papers being served upon the grandparents. The grandfather had been a long-time politician and deputy sheriff, and had served under Sheriff Naranjo and his predecessors. The case was set before the Honorable District Judge James Scarborough, and the writ provided that the grandparents produce the child at 10 in the morning.

Court was convened, and the grandparents came in with their attorney, Bert Prince, a well-known Santa Fe lawyer. Upon questioning by Judge

Scarborough, both said that early that morning their son had arrived at their home and had overpowered the grandfather, and had taken the child away to a place...they "knew not where."

Judge Scarborough leaned over the desk and said to the grandfather, "I have known you for the 20 years you've been an officer of the county, and I know that nobody, not even your own son, could ever overpower you, nor could anyone at this time. And because I know this, I'm gonna remand you to the county jail for contempt of court—until you produce the child."

My client nearly fainted. She begged me, "You can't let the judge do that to these poor old people; these grandparents can't go to jail." I said, "Never mind, this is New Mexico justice, and you do want your child, don't you?" "Well, yes," she said.

We waited throughout that day and the child was never produced. Grandma and grandpa still reposed in the county jail. Finally, at noon on the following day, the little girl was brought to court, wearing a filthy dress and with holes in her socks. Her tangled hair lay in mats. She was accompanied by at least 30 relatives, who packed the courtroom.

Judge Scarborough ordered that the custody be awarded to the mother, and he discharged the grandparents from custody. My client took her child and went back to California.

A ticket to ride

One of my divorce clients was the daughter of a very wealthy Kansas family whom I'd known for many years. She had married a struggling young artist from Albuquerque. The marriage might have worked except that they were both alcoholics and engaged in furious fights when they were intoxicated.

One time, the fight was more violent than usual: They completely wrecked a new home they'd just bought. They broke out all the windows, smashed the furniture, and used knives to rip open a custom-made, eight-foot satin damask couch. Finally, they even ripped out the woodwork. The next day, my client gathered up her husband's meager belongings, handed them to him along with a bus token, and told him to go down to the corner and catch the bus.

"Honey, you're not going to leave me like this, are you?" he cried. "Yes, you son-of-a-bitch, that's the way I got you and that's the way you're going!" she answered.

The Pirate was the booty

In retrospect, it is disheartening to recall that in several divorce matters I handled, there seemed to be greater concern about who got the foreign car or the furniture than about who got custody of the children, or how their custody would be divided. In one case, the main object of the battle was a dog.

The defendant, my client, was a brakeman on the Santa Fe Railroad. He was often gone several days at a time on a run, and then would return home. He was having trouble with his wife, and there was only one creature he loved, an English bulldog named The Pirate. The Pirate became the center of the divorce action, since the couple had little else than the bulldog, few belongings, and little property.

While my client was out on his regular run, his wife gave The Pirate away, and refused to disclose where he was. My client broke down in tears. The big, burly man wept uncontrollably over his lost pet. We never were able to get his wife to disclose what happened to The Pirate.

The Pot Creek case

I had a client who was a logger and worked in the mountains as a subcontractor for another contractor who did timber work for the Pot Creek Lumber Company. (Pot Creek is near Taos.) My client had put out the money for his labor, insurance, and had even paid the room and board of everybody working for him. He thus had a tremendous stake in the money coming to him from the main contractor, who was working directly with Pot Creek Lumber.

My client had heard rumors that the contractor, who was from

Louisiana, intended to get his check when his contract was up with Pot Creek, and to leave for Louisiana without paying any of the subcontractors. In other words, he would leave my client and others high and dry.

I prepared the petition and necessary document to seek a writ of attachment of garnishment to be served upon the Pot Creek Lumber people. I read all the statutes; I looked up all the information about how you do a writ of garnishment; I had the affidavits all prepared. Along with the seals and ribbons, I purchased the bond and took all my paperwork with me to the office.

I had a call from Johnny Simms, Jr., who was representing the Pot Creek Company. He said, "Mary, you'd better get that writ over here. Get the Deputy over here with that writ because the contractor is sitting in the outer office and unless you get that court order over here to stop it, I've got to give him his check!" Lo and behold, I had read everything in the book, but it never occurred to me that I had to take all this paperwork to the Sheriff and have him serve the Pot Creek Lumber Company, in order to preserve the rights of my client. We got hold of the Sheriff, paid him a little extra, and got the writ served in time. My man got paid, not due to my good efforts but again to the kindness of other attorneys in the field who were generous and helpful to young, ignorant attorneys (like me!).

Military maelstrom

One of the cases that I should never have gotten involved with was representing a woman who had been married to the chief of the chemical lab at Sandia Base for over 25 years.

Among her other problems, she related that her husband was an amateur photographer and for many years had maintained a studio in their home. There he photographed, in the nude, various young women who worked in whatever office he happened to be situated in at the time. Since he was in a high-security position, these photos would have provided powerful blackmail material if they fell into the wrong hands.

My client brought in a suitcase full of photographs, and spread them out on my desk. The photos were all in the sepia tones that we used to call rotogravure. They were artistically done, and in general all the models were very young women. Some had been seated in ludicrous positions and had been covered in oil, to obtain a different type of texture. I asked my client why she had allowed this to go on in her home for most of the years of her marriage. Why hadn't she complained or made some effort to sever herself from this man before a quarter of a century had passed? Her response was that "When you have a family to raise, you will do anything."

I regret to say this was a common phrase among my female clients to justify whatever activity they suddenly grew tired of and for which they finally got the courage to make a complaint and follow through on it.

The attorney for the husband got in touch with me and demanded the return of the photographs at once. I delayed returning them, frankly, so that we could negotiate a better property settlement for his wife. This couple owned a great deal of property in New Mexico, and my client had no training or skills to enable her to go back into the labor market. She had no skills to sell and had been a homemaker—this was the extent of her experience. So, I did not return the photos at once.

In retrospect, I should never have allowed the photos in my office; the husband began calling my home in the middle of the night, saying nothing but breathing heavily into the phone. I couldn't persuade his attorney to make him stop invading my home by phone in the middle of the night, almost every night.

Finally, I decided it was going to be this man or me, and it wasn't going to be me if I could help it. So I phoned the base commander and went through 49 channels before I could make an appointment to see him. I was met at the main base gate, handed from one guard to the next, and taken through great long corridors, until I was finally led to the door of the base commander.

The base commander was seated across a long room of red carpet that seemed about a quarter of a mile long. I could see that he certainly wasn't happy to waste his time on me. So went over to his desk and introduced myself, then took a sheaf of the pictures out of my briefcase, spread it fan-like on his desk, and said, "Sir, these are the young women in your secretarial pool."

The base commander turned an exquisite shade of green, and assured me that he would immediately take care of the situation. He also delicately asked that I not mention anything about our visit to anyone.

That night, I got my usual after-midnight call, but this time a voice was attached to the heavy breathing. "I hope you're satisfied; you've ruined my career. I'm being transferred to Alaska, and I hope you're satisfied!" That was the end of that.

8

Two Desert Divas, and More

Beauty and the beast

The shiny red Pontiac convertible raced down Central Avenue, with the top down, of course. It turned the corner at Fourth Street and sped by a carload of *pachucos*, who did a double-take. The woman behind the wheel had long platinum blonde hair and a wonderful figure. The carload of young men raced after the red car. When the pulled alongside the sexy blonde, she turned to look at them, blew a kiss and grinned as they groaned. The "hot babe" they pursued was actually a middle-aged woman with a grand flair and wicked sense of humor. This was only one of the pranks of one of my favorite clients, Mary Lou.

Mary Lou had been turning heads all her life. She and her sister were concert pianists, and had once worked for Florence Ziegfeld of the Ziegfeld Follies. Not only were the sisters fine classical musicians, they were beautiful women with long, naturally platinum blonde hair. In the Follies, they played twin baby grand pianos, and their snow-white hair flowed beyond their waists. Mary Lou was in the Follies at the same time as the comedian and singer Joe E. Lewis, Fanny Brice, and W.C. Fields. Her life could have been right out of a romance novel. Her husband, formerly married to a very wealthy woman, was a well-known Boston-area architect and publisher who designed and built luxury homes all along the eastern seaboard. He also was the publisher of a series of beautiful monographs on homes built of white pine. In the early 1920s, he traveled throughout the eastern states photographing and writing about classic homes.

It was love at first sight for the two, despite the huge gap between the show business world and proper Boston society, and the fact that he happened to be married at the time they met. However, after his contentious divorce from his first wife, he and Mary Lou had a very happy life together until his death in Albuquerque. Mary Lou came to me to help probate his estate, and we donated all of his papers, photographs, letters and drawings to the Library of Congress.

Mary Lou really wasn't just a glamour girl, however. She was extremely intelligent, kind, funny, and also took time to volunteer at a local hospital and won awards for her community service in later life.

Mary Lou had a collection of costumes from her career, scrapbooks, and clippings that described the Follies and her part as a pianist. Even at her age she was still a beautiful woman, and related many wonderful backstage stories about her early days with the Follies. For example, Flo Ziegfeld would not allow anything in his shows that was not absolutely perfect. In those days the pure silk body stockings that the girls wore cost $500. And, one of the beauty tips that the girls had to follow was to bathe their breasts each night in ice water only, to keep the breasts firm. Mary Lou also showed me her collection of costumes, some of which had hidden strings and panels, so you could pull on a string and a piece of fabric fell right off—I didn't get too nosy about how these were used or when.

One day Mary Lou called and asked if I knew anyone who could help move some large boxes for her. It so happened that a perfect candidate was sitting right in front of me in my office. G.H. was a tall and burly red-haired truck driver and one-time stock car driver originally from Oklahoma. He had seen some hard times. He and his parents had weathered the Dust Bowl days in Oklahoma, and were among the few families who stayed behind when everyone else set out for California. G.H. had recently fallen on even harder times, and jumped at the chance to earn a few extra dollars. He was often blunt and blustery, and could be scary with his lined face, shock of red hair and hard-set eyes. However, underneath his gruff outward appearance, he was actually quite shy, especially around what he called "the fairer sex."

We went over to Mary Lou's home. As we walked up to the door, we were greeted by the sounds of a Mozart concerto, which floated through the front door; Mary Lou was at her grand piano in her living room.

When Mary Lou opened the door, G.H. let out a small sigh—he spied the oriental carpets and antique chairs and, of course, the stunning black baby grand piano. And he was clearly taken with the curvaceous blonde in the doorway. Mary Lou fixed us all a glass of iced tea and small, delicious pastries. GH was transfixed.

She floated over to the piano and began to play the first part of Dvořák's "Humoresque." However, with a naughty smile, she began to sing, adding her own lyrics....

In her crystal-clear voice, she sang,

"Oh wouldn't it be such a lark
Goosing statues in the park
If Custer's horse can take it
So can I...
Dah...dah...dah...."

My mouth dropped open and GH turned ashy white, then bright red, and literally jumped up and stumbled out of the room. Was a dream shattered? We will never know. Before he left, he did his job—quickly picking up the boxes and moving them. Then he raced out of Mary Lou's house. It was a while before I saw him again.

Mademoiselle

While on a trip to France, one of my well-paying clients and his wife met a young French couturier. They were so taken with her fine design and sewing work that they told her they would act as sponsors, and would set her up in a dress shop in Albuquerque, where she could carry on her trade. In response to their offer of sponsorship, and the chance to open her own shop, she came to Albuquerque, naively assuming this would be a good place for her to begin her career in high fashion. Once in Albuquerque, she made, entirely by hand, complete wardrobes for my client's wife and their daughter. She also made a complete wardrobe for their daughter-in-law and her oldest child.

At about this time my clients decided to take a trip around the world, and gave "Mademoiselle" to me to take care of. They authorized a payment to her of $500 a month, bought her a sewing machine, and told me to find her a job! They suggested that perhaps she could make draperies in J. C. Penney's. Well, Mademoiselle was such an artist and there really was no place in Albuquerque where she could ply her trade and high-fashion craft. To say to her that she could make draperies in J.C. Penney's or Montgomery Wards was out of the question. She was extremely unhappy and very lonely in the strange world that was Albuquerque.

We had no French community as such in Albuquerque, and she and I had several good long talks about what to do. She, of course, felt betrayed and misled and felt she had no place to go. She felt—and rightly so—that she had been used to make a French high-fashion wardrobe for my clients' family and then had just been "dumped" in a desert wasteland with $500 a month and a sewing machine.

As we talked, she decided that more than anything, she would like to go to the West Coast, perhaps in or near Hollywood, where she could at least get work as a costume designer or could earn a living sewing costumes. She truly was a côtière, for when she designed and made a garment, she first made a perfect model of it out of muslin. Every stitch was hand-done. She did her own fabric cutting and fitting, and indeed was a true artist.

There was no apparent place for her talents to be used properly in Albuquerque. So we looked through the Los Angeles newspapers and by fortune found an ad that had been placed in the *Los Angeles Times* by Mrs. Harold Lloyd, Jr., who was looking for a French governess for her children. Harold Lloyd Jr. was a well-known actor ("Married Too Young" and "Frankenstein's Daughter") and producer at the time. Mademoiselle thought this might be a good way to get to Hollywood. So we called Mrs. Harold Lloyd, Jr. and told her about Mademoiselle and her abilities and outlined all her references. Mrs. Lloyd was enchanted with the idea, and immediately sent money for the trip, wired the plane ticket, and Mademoiselle took off for Hollywood.

Mademoiselle later wrote to say that she had become a member of the household of the dashing French actor and singer Louis Jordan—"Where at least some people speak French some of the time"—and she felt right at home there. She just could not fit into post-World War II Albuquerque, where most of us got our clothes right off the rack.

A woman's lawyer

Even up to the early 1960s, we had no public defenders, either Federal or state, so we took turns representing, by appointment of course, people who were accused of crime and were indigent and couldn't afford to hire an attorney. Since I was about the only active practicing female lawyer in and around Albuquerque, it seemed I had the job of defending every female defendant who was accused of a major crime of any kind. There were lots of cases involving women and often their crimes were even more grievous than those of the male defendants I'd dealt with.

The fire starter

One woman I defended was accused of arson. When we checked her history we found she had set a hospital on fire by lighting a fire in the linen closet. In fact, she had a long and sorry record of arson all across the country. She had been a nurse in various nursing homes in several states and had set at least six similar fires, starting in Mill Valley, California, and moving across various states until she landed in Albuquerque. An Albuquerque family was planning a vacation and hired this woman to care for an aged grandmother and a young child with polio. The woman had what seemed to be sterling references as well as her nursing ability, so the family hired her and happily went off on vacation.

As soon as they left town, she set their house on fire, and quickly "rescued" the grandmother and child. The house burned to the ground before the fire department was called. Psychiatrists who later examined the woman indicated that she really didn't want to hurt anyone—on the contrary, she wanted to be a heroine by rescuing people. She was sent to the New Mexico State Hospital in Las Vegas for treatment.

A 'paper artist'

Other women found creative ways to get by in life. One woman I was appointed to represent had a long history of "hanging paper," or forging checks, which was her way of making a living. Her children had long since been taken away by the authorities and were all in foster homes. She was currently in jail. She told me that she definitely did not want to leave the county jail.

"I was appointed to get you out of jail and back to a job," I said.

"Well, I just won't go," she replied.

She explained that she was doing regular ironing for the guys in the jail, was getting three square meals each day and medical attention, which she needed, and besides, she was in love with one of the jail trustees. So I asked her if she was willing to go before the court and advise the judge that she didn't want out of jail. I truthfully did not want the burden on my head of being unable to get her out of jail. She said she would be happy to tell the judge that she didn't want to leave.

I set up a hearing with Judge John McManus and we appeared before the court. I advised the court that my client had something she wished to say.

My client said, "Judge, I don't want out of jail because for the first time in my life I'm getting regular meals, I'm getting medical attention, I'm washing and ironing for the boys in jail and making a little money. And, besides, I'm in love with John, one of the trustees."

Judge McManus looked down from the bench and said, "Well, this is a great kind of recommendation for my jail. I'll let you stay 30 more days, but then you'll have to leave."

An impossible fee

Many of the women I represented were homemakers and nearly totally dependent upon their husbands or boyfriends. Because of this they sometimes offered to pay my fee in unexpected ways, such as with cleaning services, fresh produce, or one time, with an armadillo purse. One young client, however, completely floored me when I presented my bill. She had several of her children with her, including a black-eyed charmer about two years old. As we talked, the little boy played peek-a-boo and sang little nursery songs. My client brought the little boy close to me and said, "Mrs. Dunlap, I can't pay you, but please take my son. Julio's a good boy and won't give you any trouble." I was so shocked that I couldn't speak—a rare problem for me. After I recovered, I told her that she mustn't even think of such a thing, and there was no debt worth a child! Later I learned that in more remote areas of New Mexico, a few parents did offer their children as servants to work off debts. (I think I recall that Abraham Lincoln had to work to pay off his family's debts, in nearly the same fashion as these New Mexico people.) In fact, when I was working in Bernalillo in the 1960s, an elderly man was brought to my office with just such a story. He was from an area way out near Cabezon, and his parents had given him to another couple when he was a child, as a way to pay off a debt. He had finally wandered away from the remote ranch where he'd lived since childhood, and was brought to my office for help. Needless to say, his days of slave labor were over—but it was in the early 1960s, not the 1860s.

9

Over the Roads of New Mexico

You never could tell where work might take you. As in the case of clients without transportation, I often had to drive out to a client's area and confer with a justice of the peace there. Once in a while I'd have to drive up La Bajada Hill, to Santa Fe, hoping the car made it. Once in a while, I would take a side trip just for fun. Often the client lived in such a small town that the justice of the peace was the only law in town, and cases were handled at the justice's home. One of my favorites was a justice who came in from herding his sheep, donned his black robes, and set up court while inviting us all to have a bowl of lamb stew; he reminded me of Justice of the Peace Tom Padilla.

The cure

Sometimes because a client had no car or other means to come into Albuquerque to my office, I would drive out and confer with them at home. Our consultation might take place under a cool cottonwood tree in the front yard or over the kitchen table or even at the bedside.

One middle-aged woman called to say that she wanted to divorce her two-timing wayward husband. A few days later she insisted on speaking with me in person—especially because I was a woman, she said—about a very delicate matter. It sounded like a very common theme, a middle-aged woman who was losing her husband to a much-younger woman. However, the woman was so insistent upon seeing me that I thought there might be spousal abuse involved or that she was frightened to have her husband know that she was even thinking about a divorce. So I arranged to drive out to the woman's home, which was near Bernalillo. With much careful planning, she had found a time when her husband was away.

I was expecting to see a downtrodden or at least unhappy or distraught woman, but the woman who answered the door was anything but sad. In fact, she had a glow about her. "Mrs. Dunlap," she exclaimed, "I may not need a divorce after all!" I was taken aback for a moment, but gathered my wits and asked her to explain what had made such a big change over the last few days. She drew me close, and as I leaned in, she whispered, "the *Curandera*."

I had run across several cases where a *curandera*, who was a combination folk healer, counselor, and medicine man (curandero) or woman (*curandera*), had helped or unfortunately harmed a local person. More often than not, the person was helped or at least felt better after being blessed or treated by the *curandera*. It might be just a case of laying-on of hands or an herbal cure, or even a special blessing.

My would-be client said she had new hope about keeping her husband. She had visited the local *curandera*, who had listened sympathetically, and then gave her the solution. The *curandera* asked, "Does your husband wear a hat?" "Yes," my client replied, "my husband always wears his cowboy hat—he's very proud of it." Then the *curandera* told the woman to take a pubic hair and place it in the band inside her husband's hat. "That way, you will always be next to him and on his mind," she said.

"I did it, Mrs. Dunlap, and I know it will work!" she exclaimed. When she saw my look of disbelief, she patted my hand, and offered me a cup of tea before I headed back to town.

I never found out if the magic worked to save her marriage, I but hope it did. You never know.

The secret home of the mushrooms

One day I took a side trip up to see a client's coal mine near Cuba, New Mexico. My client, Nick Luciani, owned one of the La Ventana coal mines, located about 11 miles south of Cuba. "La Ventana" is Spanish for "window," and the area got its name from a window in the high red rock cliffs just off Highway 44 between San Ysidro and Cuba, in northern Sandoval County, north and west of Albuquerque.

La Ventana had once been a busy coal mining town (and for a short time the area also produced copper), especially after the railroad was established in the 1920s. Prior to 1880, the coal mining industry in New Mexico was small and localized, and most people used the coal only as a household fuel. When the railroad came in, coal mining turned into a commercial venture, and the growth of the railway industry also prompted the growth and operation of smelters throughout the state. Between 1917 and 1945, 26 mines and 21 prospects (the land that contained the coal) had been leased to individuals by the Bureau of Land Management.

The village of La Ventana was originally a small stagecoach stop and it remained a ranching community until coal was found to be a valuable export and commodity. The little town of Ventana had been deserted in the 1870s because of constant raids by Navajos, but after 1914, people began moving back in. Then, between 1917 and 1945, the population exploded—in 1945, around 350 single men and their satellite family groups were recorded in the vicinity. This boom was all related to the coal mines. The town had three stores, a post office (established in 1925), a meat market, a bank, a blacksmith shop, the El Nido Hotel, a cantina, a state office building, and a school. The people of Ventana came from a wide variety of backgrounds, including New Mexican Indians, Chinese, Mexican, Japanese, Slavic, and, like my client, Italian immigrants.

Nick owned a small mine and sold his coal by the truckload. The coal from his mine had a very high BTU content but couldn't be stored very well because of its slag. Because of this, most of his coal was sold on the West Coast, where it could be mixed with oil used to run ship boilers.

My visit was not for a strictly legal matter that day. Instead, Nick had invited me to see the mine where he grew his famous mushrooms. They were the most beautiful mushrooms you'd ever see, and the smallest were about the size of a teacup. Nick regularly brought in batches of these mushrooms to the office, along with a concoction he made with the mushrooms, imported olive oil, garlic, and parsley that he grew in his garden in Albuquerque. He was a colorful character and wonderful storyteller. He was also the first person I ever saw who could bone a chicken completely, even the wings.

He'd prepare the chicken with veal stuffing, and slice the final product into a delicious entrée.

Shortly before my daughter Elizabeth Jean was born, I went on a tour of the mine. I clattered and wobbled my way down into the mine with a little light on my hat, just like a real miner, to visit the mushroom bed. The pitch-dark mine had a perfect environment, which was the real secret of the special mushrooms, according to Mr. Luciani. Nick worked in a mining and lumber business with his father, who had immigrated with Nick's mother to New Mexico from Fabriano, Italy. I never knew how he came to own the mine or who taught him the secret of the mushrooms. While Mr. Luciani had several sons, none seemed as colorful as Nick himself.

A traveling salesman, or the case of the walking pans

In the days before high-speed highways and the Internet, many of the people I visited were truly isolated, particularly in the many small towns scattered around the state. The fact that they were isolated didn't deter some pretty questionable door-to-door salesmen from finding the townspeople, selling them a bill of goods, and disappearing with the cash.

One day I drove out to a little town near Espanola, to meet with a woman with a very typical tale of woe. A pot and pan salesman had sold her a complete set of pans, and then had politely asked her if she minded if he used her order to demonstrate his pots and pans to another family. It seems he had just sold out of all his wares, and thus had no other pans to show the next family. My client stressed how polite the salesman had been, and of course she didn't mind. And of course her pots and pans were never returned, nor did the salesman refund her money. Luckily she had a receipt, and we were able to find the home office and report the salesman—my client did get a new set of pots and pans, but the salesman was never caught or punished in any way and in fact might still be selling the same set of pots and pans over and over. We'll never know.

10

THE SMALL CLAIMS COURT AND BEYOND

I n May 1956 I was appointed judge of the Small Claims Court for Bernalillo County by then-Governor John F. Simms, Jr. Our understanding was that I would then run for the same office in the general election if no stronger candidate appeared to go on the slate of local Democrats.

At the time I was appointed to the judgeship, I asked the Honorable Robert W. Reidy, District Judge of the Second District, who had been a friend of mine for many years, if he would do the honors and swear me in at as Small Claims Court Judge. Well, ignorant of the proper protocol, I was advised by District Judge John McManus that *he* would swear me because he was administrative head of the court and that I should go tell Judge Reidy of that fact. Of course, I had put my foot in it, and I had to go back and tell Judge Reidy that Judge McManus wanted to swear me in as head of the court. I was really embarrassed that I had prematurely asked Judge Reidy to do so.

Judge Reidy and his wife Lois were longtime friends. Lois had been a secretary at the Legal Aid Society of Albuquerque from the time Judge Reidy and I had first become friends. (Later, she would become my secretary when I headed the Legal Aid Society in Albuquerque.) However, Judge Reidy never really quite forgave me after the swearing-in incident, and our relationship took on a certain chill ever after.

All lawyers would like to be judges at whatever level of attainment they might be able to make. There are certain benefits from being a judge, even of a minor court, which are really the dream of all attorneys. I enjoyed what turned out to be a short tenure in the Small Claims Court because I had worked very hard with others to get the Small Claims Court established. Why was another court level needed? You only had to hear a few of the many stories about the abuses committed by the various Justice of the Peace courts around the state to understand the need. Many of the justice of the peace courts had evolved into nothing more than collection agencies; most of the JPs were not licensed attorneys and had little legal training; and many infringed on individual rights in the way they collected their fines. For example, it was not unusual for an unsuspecting tourist to find himself in jail in a small town for a period of as long as he needed to raise the amount of money the JP had arbitrarily set as a fine. The fine was determined not by the "crime" but by the traveler's ability to pay. There were many, many stories of misdeeds and under the table actions by the JPs, who were often the "only law in town."

The Small Claims Court judge before me, Charles W. Chavez, had gone on to a more lucrative job as Assistant District Attorney for Bernalillo County. One of the drawbacks to becoming a judge was that many times lawyers could not afford to become judges because it amounted to a severe financial loss.

The Small Claims Court, a court of record with written pleadings, allows both parties to appear in court, and is conducted more formally than the Justice of the Peace courts. The Small Claims Court had civil jurisdiction in matters up to $2,000 and a magistrate authority for misdemeanors. Much of the business of the courts, even the district courts, came down to the Small Claims Court for settlement of legal questions. Later there would be a determination of damages with the first judgment made in our little court.

Back to the Bar

Unfortunately, I lost the general election in November 1956, after President Dwight D. Eisenhower soundly defeated Adlai Stevenson. As a result, our entire Bernalillo County Courthouse was rid of all of us rascally Democrats. Taking our places were a bunch of equally rascally Republicans, who had mysteriously appeared out of nowhere—just in time for the election. There was a very curious twist to the story of the Republican who had defeated me in the election. On December 27, he took the oath of office, while telling everyone he planned to resign shortly after the first of the year. As soon as the Republican Governor Edwin L. Mechem appointed a new

Small Claims Court judge, Republican, of course, to replace my opponent, he would resign. Oh, and there was a little matter of the dozen or so cases he had filed in the Small Claims Court just before the election. There was no comment from my opponent or for that matter the New Mexico Republican Party. This was just politics as usual in New Mexico.

Actually, at the time I didn't feel too bad about being defeated or even depressed about all the Republican/Eisenhower people taking Democratic offices all over the state and across the country. This may have been partly due to my family's early experience with a branch of the Eisenhower family, who lived in western Kansas.

I was born at home in Abilene, Kansas, next door to the Belle Springs Creamery. General Dwight D. Eisenhower's father was superintendent of the Creamery at that time. The Creamery had a whistle that blew at six am, 12 noon, and six pm, and everyone in Abilene conducted their business in harmony and directed by the whistle of the Belle Springs Creamery. My mother was quite ill at the time I was born, and when General Eisenhower's father heard about it, he ordered that the whistle not be sounded again until my mother was better. We never forgot the Eisenhowers' kindness at a particularly bad time.

A new office close to the Courthouse

I had been considerably heartened and my ego lifted by the short tenure as Small Claims Court judge, and ever after my colleagues always called me "Judge Dunlap." I decided it might be time to get a respectable office and a better address closer to the Bernalillo County Courthouse.

By this time I had acquired two big filing cases full of files, and I had a lot of books, including a beautiful 11-volume set of *Wentworth's Pleadings*, which were published in Dublin in 1799. They were still in their original bindings, even though they were well traveled and some were tattered at the edges. [I donated the *Pleadings* to the University of New Mexico Law Library when I retired from the Equal Employment Opportunity Commission, or EEOC.] I had a couple of genuine watercolors for the wall and a hall runner that had belonged to my grandmother and namesake Mary Arminta

Kramm. I also acquired, although I didn't really need him, a sort of investigator-process server. Of course, I couldn't afford him and didn't need an investigator for the cases I handled. However, he was of impressive size, a good process server, and because of some of the scrapes I found myself in, I could put him to use merely because of his massive size and his resemblance to an end for the Pittsburgh Steelers.

I went back to taking care of the clients who had stayed with me faithfully and about this time, some of the wills I had originally drawn years before began to come to probate. It is at that point that the lawyer begins to realize that he or she may have committed some sins of omission that might prove costly to his clients, or at least embarrassing. Most of them could be cured.

Luck follows lag

At this time I had a client who brought in his mother's will for probate, a will I had drawn several years before. The decedent was an old German lady who with her husband had during their lifetime acquired a considerable amount of property, blue-chip stocks, and various other assets. The estate was sizeable and a pretty impressive estate to probate in New Mexico at that time. Some years earlier my client's son had brought his mother, who was then in her late 90s, out to our farm in Corrales because she didn't like to go "uptown." I had drawn her will after interviews with her at our farm.

When his mother passed away, my client's son, who was executor under his mother's will, had gone up to the Rodey Law Firm because his mother and father had always done business with the First National Bank, and the Rodey Firm represented the bank. My client told me that he had never been in that office before, he had no connection with the Rodey Firm, and he had not consulted them in any business matter he had in his lifetime, but that he had gone to the office because the banker had told him it was necessary to see Mr. Rodey before certain things could take place in his mother's business after her death.

The son went up to the Rodey firm as requested, and signed in for his appointment. At that time the office had a long waiting room, sort of an anteroom, lined on each side by secretaries' desks. At the end of this corridor-like reception room and secretarial pool was the office of Mr. Pierce Rodey himself. Along the sides of this of the entryway were all the offices of the various younger attorneys of the firm. My client could see the layout of the office as he sat down after being told he could "see Mr. Rodey pretty soon."

As my client sat there he could see into Mr. Rodey's office, because Mr. Rodey's office was directly at the end of the reception room. He said he could see the door open, then a young attorney going in with papers. He would see Mr. Rodey always sitting there with his feet on the desk, reading a newspaper. Each time my client asked the receptionist when he might see Mr. Rodey, he was always told, "Mr. Rodey is in conference."

My client sat there for about an hour. Several times he saw the young attorneys going into Mr. Rodey's office with sheets of paper and then coming out again, and Mr. Rodey continued to read his newspaper. Finally, my client had enough, and got mad. He said he felt that this was "kind of a shabby way to treat a prospective client," and he remembered that I had drawn his mother's will. So he came over to my office. After I satisfied myself that he had not consulted with the Rodey firm, and that he had no connection with them and that there were no ethical conflicts, I accepted the assignment and took this will through probate.

It was a large enough estate and had enough assets that we needed accountants, along with tax experts, and we were able to deal with this estate in an appropriate manner and to follow through on it. Did I mention that the statutory fee was also most welcome? We were able to put that to good use, and dealing with all the various facets of an estate of that size was also a great experience.

This case indicated to me also that whether or not a lawyer gets a piece of work, particularly when he or she is a sole practitioner, is rather a matter of chance. I always was pretty good at finding new business; however, this particular case fell into my lap and was not handled through the designated firm because my client was treated rather cavalierly. I had many other clients and many were friends. I don't mean that I mixed business with any social matters, except when absolutely necessary.

Back to Pennsylvania

Among the many people who found their way to my law office were some who really lived on the far margins of society, including a real railroad hobo and a former bootlegger, schemer, and one of those persons who make you want to cross the street when you see him.

I was appointed to represent one of the last real hobos, who had lived on the road all his life. He started out in Pennsylvania, where he began working in a shoe factory at the age of nine. His job was to insert the tongues into the shoes. He had led a normal and ordinary life until his mother died. After this, he went on the road and had been moving around ever since.

It was a federal case, because the old man had been charged with theft from an interstate shipment of freight. He was arrested on a train near Vaughn, New Mexico. The old hobo was caught in the baggage car, where he had opened a couple of boxes of books and a woman's suitcase. When he was apprehended he was sitting on the boxes looking at the books and the woman's clothing. A fellow passenger was a burro that was being transported in the baggage car.

He told me that he had merely climbed in through the open doors of the baggage car, along with his bottle of Garden Deluxe wine, which was keeping him warm in mid-winter New Mexico.

Well, the first thing we did was to get a barber to go up to the jail to help clean him up with a new haircut and shave. When he was arrested he was wearing a slick old suit coat that was so dirty that it was gray all over and stitched together with twine down both sides. The man had an FBI rap sheet about eight pages long, including many small breaking and entering charges, along with petty theft, vagrancy, and other minor offenses, none of which involved use of force against a person.

I quietly borrowed one of my husband's least-favorite suits, and we bought the man a new shirt and some shoes. When he appeared in court he looked very presentable and reasonable. We told the judge the story. The man's main aim in life was to make his way back to Pennsylvania, where he was eligible for an old-age pension.

Federal Judge Carl Hatch asked the man about some of the charges on the long rap sheet—for example, the charge of stealing a watch. "Your Honor," he said, "I was only leaning on the front window of the jewelry store when the window caved in—I just picked up couple of the watches—I was admiring them and their fine workmanship when a policeman arrested me." He told Judge Hatch that he had no intention of stealing any watches—it was just an unfortunate accident.

Judge Hatch ordered the man to serve six months in the U.S. Federal Hospital in Springfield, Missouri. At the end of that time, he told the man that the U.S. Marshal would provide a ticket back to Pennsylvania. He told my client that the six months would allow him to be fed and to get his health back so he could get back on his feet.

The dirtiest man in town

Another Albuquerque street warrior who was directed to my law office was a really terrible old man by the name of William "Pop" Payne. He and his niece Mary were the bane of most of the charitable agencies in Albuquerque. Mr. Payne had come from the Black Jack Oaks country in eastern Oklahoma. Early in his life he was a bootlegger and involved in various other activities. His greatest claim to fame was that his son Donald Leroy Payne was on the FBI's "Ten Most Wanted" list for five consecutive years. Donald had a long history of sex-related crimes and was charged with rape in Houston, Texas. (The case was eventually dismissed in 1965.) Pop himself was a former inmate. One day he told me he was the only person I would ever meet who "went to prison for killing a dog."

"Now Pop," I said, "No one ever went to prison for killing a dog."

He looked at me slyly and said, "Well...it was a law dog...."

He told me had been sentenced to prison for killing a police officer in Oklahoma and was permitted to take his own commitment papers and check himself into the Oklahoma State Prison at McAlester, Oklahoma, after sentencing. And it got even better—while in McAlester, obviously with lots of time on his hands, Pop came up with a brilliant idea. He told me he had invented a "Perpetual Motion Machine." But, of course, the warden had stolen his plans, he said, and he never got any benefit from his scientific work.

Pop also was famous as one of the most unwashed persons in town—he had a real aversion to bathing, as did his niece, Mary. When Mary's skirt got dirty, she merely added a new one right on top, so she had a great, swooping silhouette with her many colorful skirts. Her dark hair was pulled back into a bun that would remind you of a flamenco dancer, and she wore two tiny spit curls, one by each ear. In summer, the sweat ran down her face below her little spit curls, making a dusty little path down her cheeks. Pop was also the bane of the county jail and drunk tank, and more than once the other prisoners dragged him over and hosed him down so they could bear to be in the same room with him.

Mary also told me about Pop's long grey coat and how they used it to rid their house of what she called "cuke-a-roach-ees." The two would drag Pop's long old overcoat into the middle of the room, and leave it lying there for a few hours. When they returned, they'd gather up the coat, now loaded with cockroaches, drag it outside and shake it over a fire in the yard. This seemed to be just another invention by Pop, and was probably an early version of a roach motel.

On this occasion the two asked me to help them with an insurance matter. Pop and Mary had insured their household goods for $4,000 and while they were away from home "buying groceries" or doing whatever errands they had, the house caught fire and burned up all their household goods. The insurance company declined to pay for the loss because they suspected arson, but could not clearly establish that Mr. Payne and his niece had any part in causing the fire.

One day the attorney for the insurance company called in a panic—"Your client, Mr. Payne, and his niece are here in my office and they want to be paid for their loss. I'll make a deal with you—if you'll come over here immediately and get them out of my office as quickly as possible, I'll give you the check for the claim." So I went over to the law office, and as promised, the attorney handed over the check. However, Mr. Payne and his niece immediately said they would not accept the check because they didn't trust the banks, anyway. They would only accept the $4,000 *in cash*. By that time the banks were closed.

To conclude this situation, the attorney for the insurance company called the bank, sent his secretary down with the check, and she was let in the back door of the bank. She came right back with $4,000 in $20 bills. I cautioned Mary that in the area where they lived, if anyone knew they had this much money, her life and safety might be in danger. She just laughed, tucked all the $20 bills in her bra and went happily on her way.

The Payne family saga continued. Mary had told us previously that her daughter Rosa had died in the New Mexico State Mental Hospital in Las Vegas after she was given "ani-mally" shots by a doctor who ran the institution. According to Mary, the doctor was actually a veterinarian and had never had a medical practice with humans, just animals.

Another of Mary's daughters had been on her way to Albuquerque from Los Angeles on a Greyhound bus and had a breakdown while on the bus. She was brought into Albuquerque and placed in the solitary cell at the Bernalillo County Jail. In those days we had no facilities for detention or care of mentally ill persons before they had a hearing to determine their sanity. There was no emergency procedure, and no holding place except the Bernalillo County Jail. So the young woman was placed in the solitary confinement cell, which had wide open access to everyone. Yes, the cell was padded, but anyone could look right in. The young woman began taking off her clothing and otherwise exhibiting herself to all passers-by, and repeatedly threw herself on the floor of the cell. When word reached him of this, Mr. Payne came to the office and asked if I would go with him to the District Attorney's office because he now had enough money to pay for a room for her at Nazareth Sanitarium, where she could get mental health care until another process could be put in place for her care.

We called upon the District Attorney, who took one look at Mr. Payne and said, "If you've got any money, old man, I suggest you take it home and use it to clean *yourself up*." Mr. Payne lunged for the DA, and it took all my strength to keep him from beating the District Attorney to a pulp and perhaps becoming the second "law dog" to get Payne in trouble.

Many years later I was waiting at a railway crossing in one of the toughest areas of town when another car rear-ended mine, tangling our bumpers and pushing our cars onto the tracks. It was getting late and no one was around. From out of nowhere came four really rough-looking men. I looked again and saw—guess who—Pop Payne among the men. "Come on boys," he shouted, "Let's get the Judge's car loose here!" With a tug or two the men freed my car and I was able to go on my way. Pop faded away into the darkness with his friends.

A man who loved Cadillacs

Mr. J, one of my clients, owned an automotive paint and body shop, and was one of the first persons in Albuquerque to have a shop for fender and body repair work. He was originally from Kansas City, Missouri, where he went back far enough that the automobiles really were horseless carriages, and the frames were made of hickory wood. He was a great lover of Cadillacs and believed they were the safest kind of car you could drive. He himself had driven Cadillacs all his life, and he actually refused to drive any other kind of car. He said that in his many years of evaluating wrecks, when a Cadillac and other car were involved, he would always find the Cadillac sitting there in the middle of the road, perhaps with a smashed headlight, but the Chevrolet or the Ford or any of the lighter cars would be totally smashed and wrapped around the Cadillac, while the Cadillac stood strong and firm.

Mr. J was a World War I veteran, a member of the 42nd Army Unit, also called the Rainbow Division, and maintained contact with the few veterans then remaining who had been friends of his in the Armed Services in France and Europe. The Rainbow Division was named in World War I by Douglas MacArthur, who at the time was a major working at the office of the Secretary of War. General MacArthur is credited with saying, "The 42nd Division stretches like a rainbow from one end of America to the other." MacArthur was instrumental in the formation of the Division and was appointed its Chief of Staff and promoted to Colonel. The 42nd (Rainbow) Division was activated in August 1917 and arrived in France that November. During its time in France the Rainbow Division participated in six major campaigns and suffered over 50% casualties.

Mr. J was becoming deaf, had a very irascible temper, and finally shut down his business and retired. He had come down from Kansas City to Albuquerque for his health, as had many other folks at that time. He said that he felt that he could no longer continue working in the body and fender business, most of which was channeled to him through insurance adjusters and various insurance companies, because of the dishonesty he had to deal with. His shop did excellent work. He felt that the car insurance industry was riddled with kickbacks, and he said even the insurance adjustor in charge of evaluating wrecks expected a kickback from him. The man from whom he bought his auto glass wanted a kickback, and the parts people also felt they should have a little tip on the side. I don't really believe all of this was 100 percent true but what was true was that the old soldier found no pleasure or enthusiasm for this particular campaign.

You can beat up the man, but leave his hat alone

I had a delightful Irish client by the name of Sullivan, who lived in the neighborhood near the office and who came by occasionally to have some of the office coffee. He was like all proper Irishmen—a little mad, a little bit emotional, and a little loud. In the summertime he wore a flat-brimmed straw hat like those you would have seen in Vaudeville, along with a white satin vest. In fact, this was the same kind of flat straw hat—along with the satin vest—that my mother told me had first attracted her to my stepfather.

Sullivan and his wife apparently were very loud, and the neighbors complained that they were continually fighting and creating a ruckus. One day Mr. Sullivan came to the office and he told me he wanted to sue his wife for divorce. I asked him to give me the particulars, and asked him why he felt he should take that kind of course after the many years he and his wife had been together. He produced his famous straw hat, which was smashed flat. In the midst of a fight, his wife had grabbed his hat, thrown it on the floor, and stomped it flat—completely destroying it. After this, he felt he had to rid himself of such a callous person, he said.

The moment passed, and Sullivan stayed married, and he came by often with new trials and tribulations. For example, he and his wife had a beautiful daughter who was a stewardess for an international airline. She was indeed a beautiful woman. However, she was a little past 30 and told me that she had begun to see the pattern of little crow's feet around her eyes so that she was going to be grounded and assigned to be an instructor in the airline's stewardess school.

Mr. Sullivan came to the office one day and told me that his mother-in-law had come from New York to live with him and his wife, but he was going to put her on the bus back to New York City. When I asked why, he said that when his mother-in-law received her Social Security check she didn't put a cent into the Sullivan household budget for her care and keep. Instead, she would cash the check and spend a good portion of it on Old Bushmills Irish Whiskey, which she drank every day, with or without coffee in it.

I assured Mr. Sullivan that no way should he place this aged woman on the bus and indeed that he knew better than to send even a dog unattended on a bus to New York City with nobody there to meet or take care of them. Instead, because of the advanced age of his mother-in-law, I assured him that we would look into a social agency that could provide a case worker to meet the bus and help the old lady find housing. Mr. Sullivan threw a small tantrum—he felt justified in throwing her out, and couldn't get over the fact that she spent all her money on Old Bushmills. I never learned what happened to her but was certain that she had to find a new address—quick.

Christ on the Sandias

I conducted a real estate closing for an elderly couple from Indiana. The husband had been a machinist for many years with Holland Furnace Company and then had retired, bringing their life savings to New Mexico. Both had serious heart conditions, but had made the long trip to New Mexico after having a vision. In a sort of religious trance, they had both had a vision of the second coming of Christ, which they said was imminent, and said he would appear on the west face of the Sandia Mountains.

These good folks had never heard of the Sandia Mountains. In fact, they thought New Mexico was a foreign country. Even so, they gathered their life savings and came out so that they would be present when Christ reappeared. They built their little home as close as possible to the Sandia Mountains. I sort of inherited this couple because they had no friends or family in New Mexico, other than the postman.

The husband passed away, leaving his wife alone and unable to care for herself because of her heart condition. We tried for some time to find live-in help for her, and it was a real challenge, for many reasons. One was that the elderly lady had reached a stage of senility where she believed that anyone who came into her home was going to steal her sheets and other bedding. She accused each helper of theft until the person in charge of sending out live-in aides grew tired of this and refused to send one more person out. The head of the Employment Security Commission informed me that she was not sending another person out to the home. It was at this point, after conferring with her, that I tried to find an appropriate nursing home for her.

Sad to relate, I couldn't find any place I could recommend. At one nursing home I visited, six elderly ladies sat in a row of six rocking chairs on the porch, rocking back and forth in a perpetual ballet. All greeted me eagerly and one lady, particularly, told me her son was the head of a government agency in New Mexico and that he was very kind to her. That is, on the first Sunday of every month, and only after church, he always came by for a visit, this loving and dutiful son.

Nobility has no price tag

I was adopted as a sort of honorary "aunt" by a family for whom I had gotten an adequate kind of a settlement out of the local gas company. Actually, the liability was so obvious that even a first-year law student could have accomplished almost the same thing. I didn't need this "adoption" because I had other honors at the time. I was already in an obscure book called *Women Lawyers in the United States*, and I was also listed in *Who's Who of American Women*, and I'd received several plaques for dedication to defending the rights of the underprivileged. I was also often asked to speak to civic groups.

My association with this family continued throughout my professional life, and we are still friends. The father of the family was a fry cook who actually under other circumstances could have been a cordon bleu chef or at least a *sous* chef because he could cook anything until it was just delicious. He could make a brace of pies with meringue with high lofting. He could do magic with a steak, and he could take a little flour and yeast and water and turn out French bread as good as any I've ever eaten. He grew up in Raton, New Mexico, and beginning at the age of 10 had worked in the mines. He worked underground, picking slate out of the coal as it came by on conveyor belts. His wife had also had a very hard childhood: she grew up in the south, the child of a very poor family, and had ruined her health at an early age by working in the cotton fields. She told me that every day she picked the cotton and then dragged a 50-pound bag of cotton behind her in the fields. This family had two grown sons, two lovely blonde twin 13-year-old daughters, and a six-month-old baby.

The family lived in a rented house that had an old Servel Gas Refrigerator that suddenly quit freezing ice. They telephoned the gas company, which sent out their repairman. He worked on the machine and pronounced it as fine. It did indeed begin to freeze ice in sufficient quantities. However, the machine should have been "red tagged" by the gas man. During the evening meal, the family became ill, and attributed the illness to the fact that they probably were catching the flu. During the night the mother awakened and was so ill that she couldn't even stand up, so she called the neighbors, asking for help. The machine had not only begun to freeze ice, but had filled the home with carbon monoxide, and all of the family was quickly hospitalized. All had suffered carbon monoxide poisoning.

Under appropriate discovery procedure, the attorney for the gas company deposed at great length every member of the family—with the exception of the baby—and later we negotiated a settlement that was appropriate and was accepted by my clients. (As late as 1988, government safety experts continued to warn consumers that old Servel gas refrigerators were leaking carbon monoxide, and that these should be used only in outdoor shelters or sheds. The gas-only refrigerators were largely used where electricity was not available, in hunting camps or vacation cottages.)

The main thing I recall about the endless depositions was that the attorney for the gas company filled the small deposition room with cigar smoke—the family had escaped one type of fumes only to be confronted with another. I decided that inhaling all this smoke must be part of the industrial injury we get for being lawyers. I was in many smoke-filled rooms, back to the days when I was really too young to be there. In this case, I always wondered if the smoking legal rascals used it as a device to hasten the settlement or at least to take all oxygen out of the room. It was sometimes so bad that we all might have been anxious to reach some agreement, any sort of agreement, to escape from those unbearable rooms.

I was never quite able to take this cigar smoke even though my husband smoked Italian stogies that were so strong that no human could smoke a whole one at one time. In fact, he said no one ever wanted to borrow one, and he couldn't finish one himself. When we asked him why he would smoke such horrible cigars, he smiled and said, "Did you ever see anyone ask to borrow one?"

Both the mother and father of this family were members of Alcoholics Anonymous, and they had decided to devote their lives, and the time they had left, to kindness and good acts towards the other folks who also were associated with AA. For example, the couple even bought a cow so they could give the milk away to children of a family who otherwise would have no milk. I was often a guest at their house.

As well as an honorary aunt, I was sort of house counsel for the family. Once I had to go to Justice of the Peace court to represent the wife because one of the neighbors was casting aspersions upon the background of one of her children. My client was so angry that he broke a limb off a nearby tree and beat the woman on the head and shoulders. I also often had calls late at night from my "nephews," who from time to time tippled a little and were driving down the road, weaving more than the local policemen patrolling that area would accept.

With all their good deeds in the face of adversity, one stood out above all. Late one night a young girl knocked on the couple's door. When they opened the door, she stood shaking, holding a tiny baby only about five days old. The mother was a young girl who had kept her pregnancy a secret from all her family members, even from her grandparents, with whom she lived. The tiny baby girl hadn't been cleaned up after the birth and her eyes and nose were full of flies. The baby was completely dehydrated and hadn't been given food or water since its birth. The girl begged the couple to take the baby, and they did so immediately. They raced the baby to the hospital emergency room.

The "baby" of the family is now a beautiful young woman, who turned out to be the star of the whole family, a terrific scholar and top professional.

Mortal combat: Two morticians and one body

I once arbitrated a dispute between two morticians that had a Dickensian twist. A client called me, in hysterics, saying that her father had just passed away and that representatives of two competing mortuaries had arrived, ready to take the body away. The two morticians were in her front yard and in the midst of a fierce argument about who was going to remove the body.

I calmed her down long enough to tell her to put mortician A on the phone and let him talk to me, and then I would talk with mortician B. The first mortician said that he had a pre-need contract that had been paid for by the deceased and that he had a contract to handle the remains. If he didn't take the body, unquestionably my client would sue him for failure to perform his contract. My client had already told this mortician that she was not pleased with the way he had handled the services for her late mother, and therefore there was no way that he was going to touch her "Daddy's body." I assured mortician A that he certainly would have a good defense, in my opinion, for impossibility of performance. ("Impossibility-of-Performance Doctrine" is a principle in contract law whereby a party may be released from a contract on the grounds that uncontrollable circumstances have rendered performance impossible.) I told mortician A that if it would make him feel any better, we would give him a release under the contract and an agreement not to sue him for his failure to perform this act—which my client would not allow him to do anyway! I then spoke with mortician B and advised him that my client wished to use his services and that she would verify this, and that it was okay for him to go ahead and remove the body and take it to his mortuary.

After the funeral services, we requested, on behalf of the estate, the return of the money that had been paid in the pre-need contract by the woman's late father. We were advised that because there were several possible heirs, the mortician's attorney would not allow his client to return any monies until such time as an administrator of the estate of the deceased had been appointed. So we went through the motions of filing with the probate court for the appointment of an administrator of the estate of the decedent. The administrator was appointed; the mortuary that did not perform under the contract gave back the money; and the matter was handled appropriately and routinely.

We let the estate die on the vine but it was a bit of an unusual mix-up with two morticians and one body.

No rest for the wicked

All Legal Aid offices have their share of cases involving crooks who prey upon the less fortunate or the unsuspecting poor. A salesman worked his way through Albuquerque's Black community selling "the right to be buried" (not a burial plot) in a local cemetery. The salesman then so "generously" threw in a small down payment, the contracts were discounted to the First National Bank, and the people quickly received payment books from the bank. The bank included a friendly note thanking them for their business and reminding them to "please make your payments on time." The phone began to ring off the hook at the Legal Aid Office and yes, we did win that one in Court.

11

You Never Know Where the Road May Lead

I had a young client for whom I had secured six divorces—yes, six, during the days when men and particularly women were ostracized for just one. I really never understood why my client bothered getting married in the first place, because most of her relationships lasted little longer than a weekend.

Husband number seven was a door-to-door vacuum salesman, and number seven turned out to be the sorriest of the lot. At the couple's rental home, the new bridegroom discovered a Social Security check belonging to a previous tenant in the mailbox. Since he was out of funds at the time, he forged the check and cashed it, then used up all the money. In due time, the Secret Service came around and hauled him off to jail. My client begged me to represent him, and I reluctantly agreed.

I had known about the family of my client's new husband for many years, and they had quite a reputation in the community. After their mother died, the children almost raised themselves on the streets. In addition, number seven had also served hard time in the New Mexico State Penitentiary. He was convicted of manslaughter after beating a man to death. So, he was hardly the Eagle Scout type we lawyers wish we had when we take such a case to Federal Court.

After a plea of guilty by a defendant or a finding of guilt by a judge or jury, the judge is furnished with a comprehensive probation report, to help determine an appropriate sentence. With this defendant's sad record an open book to the court, there wasn't much we could do in this case but try to make restitution, and for me to make a speech that might call for mercy or might attract the attention of the court to extend a little leniency toward the defendant. I certainly couldn't rely on what was generally known around the Albuquerque Bar, namely that Judge Hatch liked honest people who had good work records. This client was zero in that respect.

I paid a visit to my client's father-in-law, who agreed to advance the money for restitution for the stolen Social Security check. And, good to his word, he gave a check to the defendant to bring to the court, so we could present it to the probation department and then be able to show the court that we had done the best we could to pay back the stolen money. I carefully prepared a speech for the court, based upon the evidence that the defendant was contrite and had secured the money to repay the stolen check, and in effect that the defendant would go forth and sin no more.

We went to court. Unfortunately, somewhere between his home and the courtroom, the defendant managed to spend all the money, and he met us in the courtroom without a dime on him. My carefully prepared speech went right out the window—I had to shift gears immediately and figure out how in the world to defend him besides pleading the man guilty.

What I did caused quite a stir. My defendant entered a plea of guilty because there was no way to get around the fact that he had stolen the check, and the force of the government experts and his record offered no possible good result for this man.

In my speech to the court, with Judge Carl Hatch presiding, I turned to the defendant's background, noting that he had been raised by a neglectful father and a stepmother who was "one for the books." I pointed out that he was raised on the streets of Albuquerque, and that his stepmother barred him from the home, and as a result he fell into bad company and later into trouble. My goal was to lay a foundation that might enable the defendant to get a short stretch in La Tuna Federal Prison, a minimum security prison in Anthony, Texas, or a similar institution.

Well, as soon as I got back to my office after the hearing, I received a call from the defendant's father. He called me a despicable name and assured me that he was going to sue me for "every goddamned cent I had" and all of my property because I had berated and insulted his wife. To add to my general misery at this point, the *Albuquerque Tribune* came out with a front page article, with the following headline, 'Tragic Family' Head Given Time in Prison,' and down in the article noted that the lawyer said the stepmother was "one for the books." I knew then that I had had it.

The next blow came soon enough. The phone rang and Judge Hatch's very stiff and formal secretary said in a very cold tone, "You *will* be in Judge Hatch's office at one thirty this afternoon." Many of us were a little scared of Judge Hatch and often made less than wonderful presentations because we were in awe of the majesty and power of the Federal court. At any rate, at about one pm I went to Judge Hatch's office and literally shook in my boots for the next half hour.

When I was finally ushered into the judge's chambers I found him sitting at his desk roaring with laughter. He said, "Before today I never thought you were worth a damn, but today in my court, Madam, you were magnificent!"

Then he threw a set of keys across the desk to me and said, "I need a law clerk and I want you to come to work in the morning. He added, "Why didn't you apply for the clerkship with the court?"

I began to stammer and stutter and said, "Judge, I can't come in the morning...because, your honor, I do have some clients..." and otherwise tried to get myself out of this. But the judge continued, "Well, we'll give you a week to get rid of your clients. Now stand up and take the oath so I can get you on the payroll!"

And thus began five enjoyable years, during which I learned more with Judge Hatch in his court than all I had learned before in my practice of law. My client didn't escape justice, but received a relatively light sentence of two years in prison. Considering the charge and his background, that was far better than I had expected.

12

DAILY LIFE AT FIFTH AND GOLD

At the time I went to work for Judge Hatch, the Federal Courthouse, located at Fifth and Gold streets in downtown Albuquerque, followed a rather leisurely pace, so there was enough time to do everything in a proper and very formal manner. Congress had not yet loaded up the federal courts with the massive class action suits that would assure civil rights, or even the minute statutes, such as the one prosecuting anyone who turned back the odometer on a used car.

In those days there was plenty of time to do things properly. For example, in Judge Hatch's library we kept a complete card index of every case tried in the Tenth Circuit Court of Appeals and in the U.S. Supreme Court. This index was updated daily so that when an attorney cited a ruling case as precedent in an action, the judge was able to say to the attorney "...Yes, but, Mr. Jones, what about the case of X versus Y?" Court sessions were held in Roswell, Las Cruces, Santa Fe, Silver City, and in the main Federal Courthouse on Gold Avenue.

The Federal Courthouse at Fifth and Gold.

Separating the sheep from the goats

One thing I learned early on was that many people wanted to have their cases heard in federal court, whether this was appropriate or not. Not every case had merits or should have been heard in the federal court; however, there was an ongoing flood of people who tried their best to get their cases into a federal courtroom. For example, a person who was charged with a minor misdemeanor that would ordinarily be handled in magistrate court would demand that his case be heard in the federal court. It might be a case of speeding on a military base. The irony was that in Judge Hatch's court, at least, such defendants were asking for a world of woe; they didn't know that they were certain to receive as much of the book as could be thrown against them.

Another group of litigants insisted upon filing weird claims in order to exercise their right to represent themselves in any court in the U.S. A good example was a relative of Senator Bronson Cutting of New Mexico, who had, incidentally, served in the U.S. Senate at the same time as Judge Hatch. The Cutting family was very wealthy. However, this relative persisted in filing identical cases, badly typed by her own hand, alleging that she was being followed by carloads and airplane loads of blacks, who she said were following her everywhere she went. She attempted to sue all the law enforcement officers in New Mexico and anyone else she could think of for not protecting her against these menacing hordes. She continued to add to her list of defendants and filing *pro se in forma pauperis* and sought the process of the court to serve practically everyone on earth and in Heaven as well. (The word pauper is Latin for "poor," so *in forma pauperis* simply means filing in court in the form of a pauper or poor person. Simply put, if you are poor, you have the right to sue or defend yourself without prepayment of fees.)

Finally, Judge Hatch issued his order that no more filings might be received from Mrs. Cutting without a specific court order.

Another order the judge issued was one to exempt all the miners who worked in the Carlsbad area from jury duty because the per diem given jurors, compared with the mileage they had to cover, was so small that they couldn't afford to come to Albuquerque to attend the court.

A blue ribbon panel

At this time, Federal Court juries for both civil and criminal cases were selected by a method approved by the Tenth Circuit Court of Appeals. The method provided that in each community in the state of New Mexico a key person was selected who reputedly knew all the people in his community and who would send in a list of prospective jurors to the Federal courts. The usual procedure back then was to weed out people with obvious statutory exemptions and other exemptions that were appropriate, and to mail questionnaires to all the others. The jury commission always consisted of the Clerk of the Court and the head of the opposing political party, who put the jury list into the jury wheel. The result of this system was to bring into jury duty a "blue ribbon," or elitist group of members of the community. The others were weeded out.

Grounds of another kind

Among my other duties, I learned that it was my responsibility to see that jury members were always provided with a large urn of coffee. In one case, which involved a great deal of money and many important legal questions to ponder, and questions of fact for the jury to determine, one juror had more pressing things on her mind. The juror, a tiny lady with a great cloud of white hair, drew me aside with an important question: "What do you do with all these coffee grounds?" As I stared at her, trying to collect my thoughts enough to give an answer, she continued, "It seems such a waste to throw them away. Why don't you save them like I do and make them into little pin cushions? They make wonderful gifts." I worried a little bit about this kind of a brain serving on a jury with important decisions to make.

On another occasion, a prospective juror appeared without a coat or jacket, both of which were required before you could be selected as a juror. Judge Hatch told the man to go home and get a coat and then return for the selection process. The man didn't come back for two days and when he did appear, this time with his coat, Judge Hatch asked him where he had been. "I live in Taos, your Honor," he said, and told the judge that it took him quite a while to get there and back with a coat, especially since he didn't have a car. After this, one of my new duties was to find several men's coats in various sizes and to keep them in the back of the library for anyone who showed up without a jacket.

New Mexico Senator Carl A. Hatch.
(Courtesy of the Library of Congress.)

Judge Hatch and Harry Truman

In 1949, Carl A. Hatch had been appointed by President Harry Truman to head the U.S. District Court for the State of New Mexico, and he served in that office until his death on September 16, 1963. In many ways Judge Hatch and President Truman were very similar in personality, background, and thought. Both were self-made men, politically savvy, and hard workers. Often the two of them telephoned each other and had long conversations. Judge Hatch was known as a tough taskmaster and was just as hard on himself as he was on everyone else. He was a well-known workaholic. He came to work early and stayed late, if necessary, sometimes holding court at night to accommodate people who had come from out of town and needed to get their cases disposed of. He began court promptly at nine am, much to the consternation of attorneys from other courts, where it was unheard of to start court before ten am. In addition, the judge required everyone with preliminary motions and other matters to be present by at least 8:30 am, to get the motions and other matters out of the way before the main case began. Since our farm in Corrales was about an hour from downtown Albuquerque, his early hours made my life interesting as well!

We all also well remember the story about New Year's Day, 1960, which fell on a Sunday. Thus, Monday, January 2, 1960 was declared a holiday—but not for Judge Hatch's court. Because jury trials were coming up later in the month, he wanted to get pretrial conferences out of the way. So he scheduled court to start on Monday, January 2; the lawyers griped but the court went on. To counteract his failing eyesight due to advancing glaucoma, Judge Hatch had his proceedings summarized on a typewriter with letters more than a half inch high. He had a sharp mind and with the help of a brief summary of the case, plus a summary of applicable law, he was ready for nearly any type of case. We all worked hard—during trials the judge would write notes, and have me look up points of law or of evidence as they arose. The research had to be done during the noon recess, so the judge could use the information to rule in the afternoon. Points that arose at the afternoon session had to be researched in time for court the next morning. The judge wanted to make sure he was right in his rulings and decisions. Most lawyers could be confident about his thorough preparation.

The judge's hardworking habits probably were formed in his early years, and he was a complex and amazing man. Like me, the judge was born in Kansas, and after his family moved grew up in Eldorado, Oklahoma. His formal education ended at age 16, when he became a clerk in his father's hardware store and then a printer's devil on the town's weekly newspaper, *The Eldorado Courier*. He became a reporter and half owner of the paper. As part of his job he covered the courthouse, and he was so impressed by the eloquence of the lawyers and the drama of the trials that he left journalism for a career in law. He studied law at Cumberland University in Tennessee, and then set off on a legal career.

Judge Hatch first came to New Mexico to defend a 19-year-old youth on a criminal charge. He turned for help to the Albuquerque law firm of Patton and Bratton. Harry Patton became state attorney general that year and made Hatch his assistant soon after. Judge Hatch served in a number of offices, including as a state district judge in 1923 to 1929, before entering private practice in New Mexico.

He apparently was a self-made man and told us that he had invented portal-to-portal pay when he was a 17-year-old working in the mines near Carlsbad. He had the job of feeding, currying, and harnessing the mules that hauled out the ore. All the mules had to be ready on the line very early in the morning to begin their work, and at the end of the day when the whistle blew they were again fed, curried, and bedded down for the night—all on the individual workman's time. The judge told me that as a 17-year-old he had gone to the head of the mining company and said it was manifestly unfair that they had to do this work on their own time, plus completing about a 10-hour workday in the mines hauling out the ore.

Judge Hatch was best known, of course, for The Hatch Act of 1939. Getting the Hatch Act, which regulated the political activities of federal officials, into law took all the hard work and political savvy that he had. (A very good description of just how hard this was can be found in the archives of the New Mexico Office of the State Historian, and can be found online at www.newmexicohistory.org). It was a true reflection of the integrity and hard work that we all knew so well as we worked with him. It was a long, and frustrating political fight, but he quietly worked on, and then, when it looked like the Act was doomed, his personal appeals to President Roosevelt and refusal to be politically sidelined finally paid off.

And the judge was also a published poet. He once wrote a poem for me that I greatly treasure. The main theme of the poem which was that he could not understand how I could wear so many hats.

The poem, written on the judge's official stationary, on Christmas Day, December 25, 1959, was as follows:

To Mary Dunlap—lawyer,
Phi Beta Kappa, wife and
Mother, too.
How can you find the time,
O woman,
So many things to do?

He was, of course, also a very powerful man and enjoyed all the various benefits of his office as well. For example, one time he became annoyed with the tap, tap, tapping of us women who wore high-heeled shoes and tapped across his hardwood floors all day every day. Thus, he carpeted the courtroom floors. Since the judge and I were the only coffee drinkers in the office, he decided it would only be fair for us to share equally in the cost of the coffee, the coffee creamer, and the sugar. He kept careful accounts of exactly what the coffee and all the other ingredients cost, and I paid my half every time, down to the penny. However, it was also my duty to go to the grocery store and buy the coffee, cream, and sugar when needed.

While the horse races were on at the annual State Fair, Judge Hatch also prepared a daily racing sheet—he plotted the races, the horses expected to win, place, and show, and said that he learned to bet on the races while he was a senator in Washington, DC.

His cool and detached secretary, Thelma Gee, who had a good understanding of stocks and bonds, was the one who covered the Stock Market circuit for the judge and spent time at the Merrill Lynch Company watching the ticker tapes come down. The judge never lost a dime on the horse races. In fact, he made a little bit of money and early on he taught me that even a small return was to be carefully calculated, and was valuable. For example, one day I told him that my father had bought a bunch of dollar stocks during an oil boom in Texas, and that most of the companies were defunct. However, I occasionally got a small dividend check after my father's death. The judge pointed out that even though these checks were small, they represented a pretty good piece of capital investment, and I should regard them more seriously than before.

Judge Hatch and Clerk of the Court Sam Byers draw names from the jury wheel.

Finding Mr. Reeves

When the Encino Medical Plaza Complex was being built, very close to Judge Hatch's home, the judge returned home one night and looked out his study window to discover that a huge utility pole had been put up on a corner of his property. No one at the utility company had tried to get his permission before this eyesore was put up right outside his study window.

The judge came to the office the next morning and told his secretary to "get Mr. D.W. Reeves on the telephone at once." Mr. Reeves was the President of the Public Service Company of New Mexico. Mr. Reeves' secretary calmly informed Judge Hatch's secretary that Mr. Reeves was at his summer home on Martha's Vineyard. Not satisfied with this report, Judge Hatch told his secretary that he didn't' give a damn where Reeves was, he wanted him on the telephone! It is reported that since there were no telephones on the Vineyard at that time, a boat was sent out to get him, and it brought Mr. Reeves back to the mainland and to a telephone. In about an hour, the light pole was gone. This was another good illustration of the power of the Federal court in private and public business.

Where's the beef, Mr. Belli?

We also had a rare visit from the flamboyant San Francisco defense attorney Melvin Belli. During the early 1960s Judge Hatch tried some of the very first million-dollar judgment cases in his court involving personal injury and death. This was also the period of time when lawyers really began using demonstrative-type evidence and props.

We had been introduced to this idea by Melvin Belli after he traveled to Albuquerque to conduct a special demonstrative evidence workshop. We paid ten dollars apiece to hear how he had used graphic demonstrative evidence in various jury cases. In one case, he had won an exorbitant award in damages for a young airline hostess who had been injured while riding in a speedboat. After the speedboat crashed, she lost both legs. Belli told us how he had brought into the courtroom a package the size and shape of a severed human leg, wrapped in white butcher paper. He tossed the package on the counsel table, which brought a gasp from everyone in the courtroom. Of course, the "evidence" was just a big piece of raw beef.

A hard man to replace

Another interesting and challenging time involved the judge's selection of a bailiff to replace William Slaughter, a long-time bailiff who had served Judge Hatch and several federal judges before Judge Hatch's time. Bill Slaughter was a member of a unique family from Santa Fe, one of the few black families in Santa Fe at the turn of the century. Bill's father and mother, William J. and Mary Slaughter, had eight children. His sister Valdera was a star student and their eldest son was valedictorian of the class of 1905. Unlike many other places in New Mexico and throughout the U.S. at that time, Santa Fe's schools were not segregated.

We all loved and respected Bill, and he was an important member of the court. As bailiff, Bill was generally responsible for locking and unlocking the courtroom and for screening visitors and materials entering the courtroom. As a law enforcement officer, he was also responsible for maintaining order in the courtroom, preventing anyone from approaching the bench without the judge's approval, preventing disturbances and smoking, and enforcing courtroom rules of behavior. He had to escort defendants to and from the courtroom, and took custody of convicted and sentenced defendants and transported them to holding or correctional facilities. A bailiff calls the court into session, announces cases and witnesses, and closes the court. In addition, he or she posts the case schedule, answers telephones, maintains courtroom supplies, and collects evidence from attorneys. In some cases, the bailiff passes verdicts from the jury to the judge and administers the oath to witnesses.

The selection of a new bailiff after Bill's death was a complicated process. The judge was looking for a black candidate who was, in the judge's words, "as white as the driven snow but who had never drifted." The selection began with contacts in the black community, who were asked to find someone who was really acceptable to blacks and whites alike and someone who had the background and sensitivity to make a good bailiff and chauffeur, for that was one more of the bailiff's duties. The effort in this sensitive search was similar to seeking a bride suitable for a king, or like going through a thoroughbred stud book to find a candidate who would fit all the minute and lofty qualifications.

I was sent to make inquiries about all candidates, to check all public records and background records, to study police records, and finally to talk to ministers of the two leading churches in Albuquerque. I talked with the precinct people and thoroughly checked out all the candidates. One candidate emerged, and seemed to be the top runner in the competition. Unfortunately, his father, who was a bailiff for one of the state court judges, had the temerity to call Judge Hatch at home to spell out in great detail all the virtues of his son. Judge Hatch resented the intrusion into his private space and as a result he didn't select this particular man, who would probably have been a very fine bailiff. It just sort of illustrates that no one can tell for sure just why he or she wasn't chosen for a job. Many factors remain unknown in the quest for any goal.

Careful sentencing

One of the most difficult tasks Judge Hatch faced was to sentence convicted defendants to terms in an institution or to probation, and to determine what would be an appropriate sentence. This is true for all judges, but Judge Hatch approached this part of his work with particular care. He studied all records, to try to determine from the pre-sentence reports (furnished by the probation department) an appropriate disposition of every single case. He often remarked that perhaps one heavier sentence would "be the straw that finally broke the old camel's back." He firmly believed that the length of the term to be served was no deterrent to further criminal activities. He also believed that the certainty of punishment was the real punishment and he deplored the use of mandatory times set for certain crimes. For example, he felt that in the case of drug dealing there was not enough flexibility and the bad situations had actually made bad laws, including mandatory sentences. He often felt physically ill because he worried all week about what to do with individual defendants.

Once I asked him how he could go on the bench when he was obviously ill. He replied sharply, "Didn't you ever try a lawsuit when you had a bellyache? Help me button up my damn robe, and let's go!"

From Slavery to Red Chief

During the time I worked with him Judge Hatch tried many interesting and important cases. For example, he tried the first case of slavery in the U.S. after the Civil War era. The case was a criminal charge brought against a trading post owner in the Grants area.

Buck Wilcoxon owned a trading post west of Albuquerque, on Highway 66, the two-lane blacktop highway that ran from Illinois to California. All along Route 66, every few miles travelers would see billboards touting the "World's Largest Rattlesnake," "the Deepest Well this Side of the Rockies," and the various virtues of Burma Shave.

Mr. Wilcoxon was charged with having enslaved an old Navajo man, Juan Largo ("Big John"). Wilcoxon chained Big John up in a dog collar and kept him tethered to a tree out behind his store. He then advertised that tourists could "See a Genuine Savage Navajo."

Mr. Wilcoxon was found guilty and sentenced to the New Mexico State Penitentiary in Santa Fe. While he was serving his sentence, Mr. Wilcoxon's son was driving his pickup on the reservation. The young man stopped to stretch, and got out of the truck. From out of nowhere a thirty-ought-six bullet struck the young man between the eyes, instantly killing him. His assailant or assailants were never found. This case was a good illustration of the inexorable fate that reached out often to people in New Mexico. Maybe everybody has his kharma and maybe whatever goes around, comes around, but it seems to come around with more visible certainty in New Mexico than any other place I've lived.

When Mr. Wilcoxon was released from the penitentiary, he came to Judge Hatch's court and asked to see the judge. In those days there was no security, no security guards or video screening before you could be admitted to the courtroom and offices. When we saw him, we immediately called the U.S. Marshal, who accompanied Mr. Wilcoxon in to visit the judge. Mr. Wilcoxon intended no harm to the judge. In fact, he just wanted to talk to him. He told Judge Hatch that the judge was the first person in his life who had ever directed him about what he could or could not do. Of course, the death of his son also had had a very sobering and sad effect on this man.

Shady business

A local businessman was charged with interstate transportation of pornographic movies, which were regularly shown at stag parties. As a real sign of those times, Judge Hatch cleared the courtroom and no women were allowed on the jury. This well-known businessman, who had used some of the capital assets from the porn sales, was found guilty. Not long afterward, in a totally separate case, the local postmaster in Alameda was also found to be involved in pornographic sales; it was ironic that the post office was located very close to the Nativity of the Blessed Virgin Mary, a beautiful and busy Catholic Church on north Fourth Street.

On another very memorable day, at least for me, my young daughter,

Mary Kay, made a rare visit to the court. Unfortunately, I hadn't checked the docket for the day beforehand. Mary Kay saw a group of young women her age sitting on the front row in the courtroom and went over to join them. When I looked for her, a little later, though, she and all the young girls were gone. It seems that the U.S. Marshal had come up to the young girls, and when he said, "All you young women come with me to my office," my daughter had dutifully gone right along with the group. It turned out, as the judge's stern-faced secretary would remind me for the rest of my days, that the young women were all prospective witnesses in a huge Mann Act case (the Mann Act is also called The White Slave Traffic Act). The young girls were all prostitutes and were in the Marshal's office preparing to testify. Luckily I retrieved my daughter before the witnesses were called, for she had already signed the witness form. And, because of the judge's poor eyesight due to advancing glaucoma, he hadn't seen her sitting in the front row with all the other witnesses.

Beyond the Reservation

The Federal Court's jurisdiction also extended to the Indian reservations, and during my time with Judge Hatch, the court handled 14 major crimes that occurred on reservations throughout the state.

The Tribal Court had the primary authority in these crimes and the jurisdiction to handle them. However, by statute and by the consent of the Indians, these crimes were turned over to the Federal Courts to be handled, usually because the Tribal Court felt they were not equipped to do so. As today, American Indians could not buy liquor on the reservation, and liquor plays a part in some of the more savage murders and injuries and mayhem that occurred upon the reservation.

Even though it was against the law to sell or provide liquor to the Indians, liquor was just as available to Indians as deep-shaft bourbon was available to all of us in Kansas during the days of Prohibition. The way it worked was if an American Indian ordered a drink, he or she was generally taken to the back room of the bar or restaurant and told to drink the pint of whiskey or wine right there. As long as the booze was in him and not on him, nobody would be prosecuted for having furnished the brew. Many of the crimes that resulted were particularly savage and very difficult to handle, for everybody involved. It was difficult for the investigative people and difficult for the Indians themselves, who had to appear as witnesses in the court.

In one case, an Indian man in one of the pueblos had shot his neighbor to death. His defense was that this neighbor had warned him that unless he did something concerning some property, he and the neighbor would turn the defendant into a rattlesnake. The defendant truly believed this could happen because his neighbor was a member of a snake clan. The defendant believed his neighbor did have the power to turn him into a rattlesnake if he didn't do what he wanted. Everyone from the tribe connected with the case outwardly denied there was such a thing as a snake clan, but we believed that the snake clan did exist. The Indians, however, needed to protect against having the fact that the clan or cult existed made public.

On another occasion, a tourist or traders had broken into the *kiva*, a sacred building, at one of the pueblos and had stolen the ceremonial feathers and other fetishes. The thieves were apprehended, but the pueblo elders refused to have the thieves prosecuted. Their reasoning was that the stolen items were religious objects and could not be brought into court, to be spread out before the public eye during the trial.

A modern-day "Red Chief"

With all the very serious cases heard in the court, now and then a funny one would come along. We had one case that rivaled O'Henry's *Ransom of Red Chief*. In O'Henry's famous short story, two thieves plan to kidnap the son of an important citizen. They demand a ransom of $2,000, collect the payoff, and are on their way. However, once they kidnap the young boy, their plans unravel as the redheaded brat takes over and refuses to leave. They just can't get rid of him.

In our modern-day version, two lifers had escaped from the Joliet, Illinois prison and were passing through Albuquerque when they noticed a teenager seated in a brand-new Cadillac stopped at a stop sign. They needed a set of wheels, and this Cadillac looked like a very likely possibility. So they told the boy to move over, jumped in the car, and sped off. The boy was the son of an oilman from Oklahoma who was in town for a business meeting. The oilman had let his son have the car to drive around until the meeting was over. Eventually the men were caught and brought to trial.

One of the co-defendants testified about their futile efforts to get rid of the young man, who didn't want to return home. As soon as they had reached the Albuquerque city limits, they told the boy to get out and get on back to Albuquerque and his father. The teen refused to leave. He was bored with school and tired of his dull teenage life and thought he'd like to join up with the men and live a much more exciting life of crime. At any rate, they took the boy with them, asking him at each stop to get out. He refused. Every time they approached a town, they pleaded with him to call home, and he continually refused. Finally, when they reached Wichita, Kansas, they drove to the bus station, telephoned the boy's parents in Oklahoma City and said, "We're paying your son's bus fare home. We're putting him on bus number so and so and we've told the bus driver not to let him off en route." Finally rid of the boy, they had gone on their merry way until the law caught up with them.

The two men were charged with kidnapping and interstate transport of a minor. The co-defendant testified that he had spent most of his 35 years either in foster care or in one institution or another. He also pointed to his very large nose, which rivaled that of Cyrano, and told the court, "Anyone with a horn like this can't be expected to amount to anything."

13

Colossal Cases

A fateful car crash

One of the largest cases Judge Hatch tried involved a large damages award, in fact an award greater than had ever been seen in a New Mexico lawsuit. A very wealthy Texan and his friend were en route from Lubbock, Texas, to go to the quarter horse races at Ruidoso Downs. As they drove along, both took swigs out of bottles of Jack Daniels whiskey. As they were headed west, at high speed, they overtook a truck and passed it on the right side, swinging down into a ditch and throwing gravel all over the truck. The truck driver related later in the trial that he had known something bad would happen to this pair. In fact, their car had disappeared over a hill and the driver said he saw a huge cloud of dust and in a few moments came upon a terrible accident.

After the car came back up onto the highway, the convertible had veered across the midline of the highway and crashed head-on into a small pickup truck. The truck carried a family of eight, a husband and wife and their six children. Four of the children were riding in a makeshift lathe and canvas shelter in the back of the pickup and two children were with their parents in the cab of the little truck. Most of the family members were killed outright, and the truck driver related on the stand how he had held in his arms a young woman who had been thrown—along with her brothers and sister—out of the back of the pickup truck. Her young baby had also been thrown out and into the bushes, but nobody could find the baby. The truck driver testified that he had promised the young mother as she was dying that he would find the baby and care for it. He later related that he found the baby some 50 yards away in the bushes, and the baby did miraculously survive.

Because of the size of the case and the many injuries and deaths, the case was divided into four parts. Here is how the outcome was described:

Barnes v. Smith, 305, F.2d 226 (10th Cir. 1962)

Wrongful death and personal injury actions arising out of collision between a pickup truck and an automobile. From judgments of the United States District Court for the District of New Mexico, Carl A. Hatch, Chief Judge, appeals were taken. The Court of Appeals, Lewis, Circuit Judge, held that award of $400,000 to a 12- year-old boy who sustained severe and permanent brain injuries resulting in loss of memory, loss of intellectual functioning, loss of orientation in space and time, difficulty in chewing, swallowing, talking and breathing, partial paralysis and injury to both arms and legs and many other difficulties, was not excessive.

These four cases, consolidated both for trial and on appeal as containing common questions of fact and law, resulted from a highway disaster involving the collision of a pick-up truck transporting a family of eight and a late-model Cadillac containing two men. The accident occurred July 2, 1960, at a point about eight miles east of Tatum, New Mexico, and caused the deaths of both the driver of the Cadillac, Houston Smith, Jr., and the driver of the pick-up, Daniel W. Barnes, and also the death of four passengers in the pick-up, Mrs. Barnes and three of the Barnes' children, Daniel, Jr., Sandra and Gloria. A fourth child, Gerald, suffered massive injuries and the remaining passengers, the son-in-law Bruce G. Jolly (husband of Gloria) and the infant Susan Jolly, suffered severe injuries.

The causes were tried in the United States District Court for the District of New Mexico after removal of Nos. 6765 and 6766 from the New Mexico state court and transfer of Nos. 6767 and 6768 from the United States District Court for the Western District of Texas. Jurisdiction in each case was based upon diversity of citizenship. In each case the executrix of the estate of Houston Smith, Jr., was defendant below.

After trial to a jury verdicts were returned favoring plaintiffs in each instance and judgments upon such verdicts were entered as follows:

In No. 6765:

> *For the death of Daniel W. Barnes, $25,000*
> *For the death of Elsie E. Barnes, $20,000*
> *For the death of Daniel W. Barnes, Jr., $15,000*
> *For the death of Sandra M. Barnes, $15,000*

In No. 6766:

> *Bruce G. Jolly (injuries and expenses), $50,000*
> *Susan A. Jolly (injuries and expenses), $1,000*

In No. 6767:

> *For the death of Gloria Jolly, $25,000*

In No. 6768:

> *Gerald W. Barnes (injuries and expenses), $ 400,000*

The plaintiffs appeal from all judgments except those for Bruce G. Jolly and Gerald W. Barnes. The defendant appeals from the judgment in favor of Gerald W. Barnes. Since the latter appeal contains but a single contention, a claim that the judgment is excessive in amount, we give it first attention for it reaches the subject matter of a contention common to the remaining appeals, that is, that those awards are inadequate. The trial court denied new trials after giving the fullest of consideration to the claims of the parties respecting both excessiveness and inadequacy.

Two mining giants

One of the last important cases Judge Hatch tried, and one that I believe contributed to his retirement and possibly his death, was a lawsuit that ran longer than most Broadway plays. In the 1960s the judge tried a case for six months, day and night. The case concerned the various rights of multiple parties to uranium right or deposits in the Grants, New Mexico area.

This was the *Homestake Mining Co. v. Mid-Continental Exploration Co., 282 F.2d 787 (10th Cir. 1960)*. This case had every kind of question of law concerning mineral rights and involved lands owned by a variety of people—Indians, Federal enclave land, State Bureau of Land Management, and private owners. The parties involved were multiple, including the

Mid-Continent Oil Company, the Homestake Mining Company out of South Dakota, Rio de Oro Mining Company, and a lady named Stella Dysart. Early in the 1920s or 1930s, Stella Dysart had gone through the area and negotiated mineral leases to at least some of the land involved in the Grants, New Mexico and Fence Lake, New Mexico uranium deposits, and received 17.5% royalties on profits. For a time the courtroom even featured Raymond Burr, the actor who played Perry Mason in the television series, because he had some fraction of an interest in the outcome of the case.

The case was beautifully tried by fine attorneys from all over the United States and New Mexico, including John Robb from the Rodey firm. The case also involved attorneys like Chester Davis from One Wall Street, who later was involved with the Howard Hughes estate. Every morning, Mr. Davis brought in fresh flowers and boxes of chocolates for all the women court attendants and reporters. The expert testimony was fascinating. Mining experts came from South Africa and engineers from many areas came in to describe the kind of mining procedures that were done in the diamond mines. They contended that the same kind of engineering and mining methods that were used to mine and produce the yellow cake from the uranium around Grants were being used in the South African diamond mines. Experts from the Sullivan Mining Company in South Africa reminded me that one of our early friends from our small hometown of Eureka, was now an executive with Sullivan Mining Machinery Company in Johannesburg. He had changed his name from Ceecil ("Ceesill") to Cecil ("Sesil"), and had evolved into a very proper Britisher in accent, appearance, and dress.

During this trial, Judge Hatch, with his prodigious memory, made only one small error of fact in a statement from the bench. I knew he was going to make it but there was no way to prevent it and nobody noticed—but I nearly got fired because of it. We had a daily record of the proceedings, which involved court reporters recording testimony in 15-minute blocks. One set of reporters would be replaced by another set of reporters while the first group went out to transcribe the material they reported. Every night at midnight, a complete record and transcript of the day's proceedings in the court had to be furnished to all attorneys for the parties and were delivered to their hotels around the city or wherever they were staying. Then, at seven the next morning, Judge Hatch and all his court personnel, including me, gathered in his chambers, where we read to him the entire record of the day before. We did this in part because of his very poor eyesight—reading was very difficult for him. In this way, everything would be fresh in his memory when he began the proceedings again at nine in the morning.

It was a killer of a case for all of us, and we were all like a bunch of legal zombies by the time the case was over. At one point we decided—that is, the judge decided—to vary the extremely monotonous situation where we went day after day and many nights after supper to hear more testimony. The judge decided to move the Court up to the federal courtroom in Santa Fe. This move involved a veritable caravan of reporters, court reporting machines, personnel, and anything the judge might need. We soon found that the altitude in Santa Fe, though not much higher than that in Albuquerque, was intolerable for the judge, so we had to turn around and come back down to Albuquerque, retracing our steps and our caravan, which looked a little like a traveling show troupe.

Initially, the case was decided in favor of the defendant, Mid-Continental Exploration Co., and was appealed. Here was the outcome:

Homestake Mining Co. v. Mid-Continental Exploration Co., 282 F.2d 787 (10th Cir. 1960)

Actions, consolidated for trial, to determine parties' rights in the mining and milling of uranium ore. The United States District Court for the District of New Mexico, Carl A. Hatch, Chief Judge, entered judgment adverse to certain parties, and they appealed. The Court of Appeals, Breitenstein, Circuit Judge, held, *inter alia* (among other things, or only one part of many), that, where the consolidated actions raised every question affecting rights of every party, the two judgments would have to be consistent as to ore obtained under lease, and, therefore, requirement that reserve unmined or stockpiled ore adequate to meet commitments of contract with Atomic Energy Commission must be reserved would have to be contained in both judgments in view of fact that it was contained in one such judgment, and that, where general partners of limited partnership for mining and milling of uranium ore had right to enter into similar ventures with others, limited partners, who silently permitted general partner to expend $17,000,000 for mill construction, mining development, and working capital in another venture of which they had knowledge, but which was hazardous and speculative, would not, after other venture had proved successful, be entitled to have general partner made a constructive trustee as to them but would be barred by laches from making claims as to such other venture.

Motion for substitution of party was denied, and judgments modified and, as modified, affirmed.

The judge goes missing

One Thursday afternoon, when the case of the day had been settled and there were no other scheduled proceedings, Judge Hatch did not return from lunch—he had gone off somewhere and we couldn't find him anywhere. His chauffeur and his secretary called his home and of course, he was not there. However, after hours of calling and worry, we had our answer.

It turned out that the judge decided to take a holiday from the Court. I learned that that he often disappeared on these little jaunts, riding all around town on the nearest city bus. He liked to get aboard and ride around Albuquerque anonymously for three or four hours, to soak up the "real world" of Albuquerque that existed outside his lofty world of the courtroom.

Epilogue

The Little Room Where No One Goes

Mary M. Dunlap on a rare vacation in Puerto Rico.

Our mother was an extremely private person, despite her open and friendly nature and love of people. She moved easily through the world and could meet a camel driver in Cairo as easily as an old friend on the streets of Eureka. But she also loved solitude and was at the same time a private person and, as she once told me, she had "a little room where no one goes." This was her own internal sanctuary, and indeed she needed that little room at many times in her life. She needed it early on, when her father deserted the family, and later with an ever-crueler, physically and emotionally abusive stepfather, struggles against discrimination as a female lawyer in a male-dominated community, and hard years balancing a family, farm, and life as a farm wife with the high standards she set for herself as a lawyer. She needed a way to escape. Late in her life she faced illness, financial challenges, raising a granddaughter, and the fact that her cancer might return at any point.

The "little room" must have been filled to the rafters by the time the drunk driver's car plowed into her car.

This book represents only a small portion of that full life, her early years in Albuquerque. She recorded only 12 tapes, for the project was cut short by her sudden death one night in 1984. On July 12, 1984, she and her granddaughter Lisa were driving home from a Commodores' concert, down Central Avenue. She loved Lionel Ritchie's music, and couldn't resist the rare chance to see him in concert in Albuquerque. As their car passed San Pedro and Central, a drunken driver in a speeding van plowed into the driver's side of her car. She was killed instantly. Luckily, her granddaughter had only minor injuries. Thus, and ironically, her time in Albuquerque ended with a violent act, just as it had begun 37 years earlier.

Her friends were stunned, and Professor Dorothy I. Cline so much so that she couldn't bear to come to the funeral. Dr. Cline wrote me soon after, saying, "Mary was not only a very competent lawyer, she was one of the most selfless persons I have ever known. If she thought of herself and her own interests, it was an afterthought. I often tried to persuade her to do something for Mary once in a while, but never succeeded. Moreover, she was so honest, she belonged in another world—not one dominated by greed, unethical practices, and hypocrisy. She had ambitions for other people: her incentives had nothing to do with competitiveness. Instead she exhibited the cooperative spirit of some of the pueblo Indians. I shall miss her a great deal, yet I suspect she did not appreciate just how much some of us would wish she had stayed with us a little longer."

This book covers just a little of Mary M. Dunlap's career, which spanned many more years and many more clients. We were able to capture just a little of it all. The following came from her very first tape as she was snowed in on Thanksgiving in Placitas. As she started recording the first tape in the mountains, she looked out upon a snowy Placitas morning, and shared it with us:

Thanksgiving Day, 1983. Placitas, New Mexico

A couple of days ago, winter blustered in, with the wind sighing around the chimneys, bringing with it a lot of snow. We are snowbound.

The way I feel about winter is that it is like an eight o'clock dinner guest who suddenly appears at 6:30 and finds his hostess still in pink plastic curlers and with nothing ready for him. We knew that winter was coming. We have a whole wall of cedar and piñon firewood along the portal. We had cleaned up all the garden. We had planted all the garlic and covered it nicely with golden straw. We had cleaned out our chimney. Yet we were still not ready for winter to come and catch us.

There are five chickadees picking on tortillas on my "tortilla tree" in the snow and a bluebird attacking, in a kind of useless fashion, an ancient bagel on top of a post.

My favorite saddle in the Sandia Mountains, where the aspens first become light green in spring and are the first mountain gold in the fall, now are not visible at all. In their place we see only the green pines and other evergreens, frosted very like a wedding cake, with snow and ice on all.

On July 18, 1984, at about noon, a small plane flew over that same saddle of aspens in Placitas, now bright green from the summer rains. It swooped in long arcs and circles, like a lazy hawk in the warm summer air, scattering the ashes of Mary M. Dunlap into eternity. Her indomitable spirit lives on.

—Mary Kay Stein

References

Chapter 1. 1947: Welcome to Albuquerque

June 4, 1947 *Albuquerque Journal*, "Parents of Five Children Die in Double Shooting"

June 5, 1947 *Albuquerque Journal*, page 1, "Woman Warned Before Slaying"

Agnes Morley Cleaveland, quotation, from *No Life for a Lady*, University of Nebraska Press, 1977.

Chapter 3. Our New World

News and ads from the daily news, courtesy of the *Albuquerque Journal* archives, 1949-1950.

Story about the case where two women lawyers were opponents, "'Ladies Day Case Is Cancelled Here," *The Albuquerque Tribune*, May 2, 1957, p.6.

Chapter 4. Beginnings

Background information about and photos of the Greenwood Hotel, courtesy of the Greenwood County Historical Society; see also the website, http://www.greenwoodhotel.org/History.htm (current at time of publication of this book)

Information about Eureka High School and activities from the late Harry A. Paulson, Minta Mary McDonald's classmate at Eureka High School, July 1990.

Chapter 5. Corrales

Information about the acequia irrigation system in the Rio Grande Valley and Corrales from "The History of Agriculture in the Corrales Valley," compiled by Mary Davis and Sayre Gerhardt, and available at: http://www.corrales-nm.org/history.htm. (current at time of publication of this book)

Chapter 9. Over the Roads of New Mexico

General background information about La Ventana and its mines, courtesy of the New Mexico Historical Society.

Chapter 10. You Never Know Where the Road May Lead

"Mary Dunlap Reported Studying Court Race," *Albuquerque Journal*, March 6, 1956, p. 2.

"Know Your Candidates. For Small Claims Court Judge," *Albuquerque Journal*, November 1, 1956, page 2.

"Attorney's Plea Fails. 'Tragic Family' Head Given Term in Prison," *The Albuquerque Tribune*, August 12, 1957, p. 1

"Hatch Names Mrs. Dunlap, "*The Albuquerque Tribune*, September 13, 1957, p. 21.

Chapter 11. Daily Life at Fifth and Gold

Some background information about Carl A. Hatch's early career and Senate career, including the writing of the Hatch Act of 1939 courtesy of the New Mexico Office of the State Historian.

Chapter 12. From Slavery to Red Chief

Some details on the Mid-Continent ruling from "Hatch Ruling in Suite Favors Mid-Continent, *The Albuquerque Tribune*, February 9, 1959, page 1.

Information about Judge Hatch's rulings courtesy of the Federal Courts of the Tenth Circuit, a list of cases, with thanks to Greg Townsend, Branch Librarian, Tenth Circuit, U.S. Courts Library.

"In Memoriam of the Honorable Sam G. Bratton, Honorable Carl A. Hatch, Honorable Waldo H. Rogers." Proceedings of the Annual Judicial Conference, Tenth Circuit, Santa Fe, New Mexico, June 29, 30, and July 1, 1964. Chief Judge Alfred P. Murrah presiding.

Epilogue: The Little Room Where No One Goes

Letters and interview with Emeritus Professor Dr. Dorothy I. Cline, Albuquerque, New Mexico, 1984 and 1986.

INDEX

www.ingramcontent.com/pod-product-compliance
Lightning Source LLC
Chambersburg PA
CBHW021405090426
42742CB00009B/1010